N o

Frank Mc Nutty
July 1992

PRIESTHOOD TODAY:
An Appraisal

Thomas P. Rausch, S.J.

D0831662

PAULIST PRESS

New York and Mahwah, New Jersey

Library of Congress Cataloging-in-Publication Data

Rausch, Thomas P.
    Priesthood today : an appraisal / Thomas P. Rausch.
       p.   cm.
    Includes bibliographical references and index.
    ISBN 0-8091-3326-1 (pbk.)
    1. Priesthood. 2. Catholic Church–Clergy.   I. Title
BX1912.R38 1992   92-747
262'.142–dc20   CIP

Published by Paulist Press
997 Macarthur Boulevard
Mahwah, New Jersey 07430

Printed and bound in the
United States of America

CONTENTS

For the priests and people
of the Diocese of Raleigh
with gratitude

ABBREVIATIONS

Documents of the Second Vatican Council are abbreviated according to the first two words of the Latin text: thus:

CD   *Christus Dominus:* Decree on the Bishops' Pastoral Office in the Church

LG   *Lumen Gentium:* Dogmatic Constitution on the Church

PO   *Presbyterorum Ordinis:* Decree on the Ministry and Life of Priests

SC   *Sacrosanctum Concilium:* Constitution on the Sacred Liturgy

UR   *Unitatis Redintegratio:* Decree on Ecumenism

Other works cited:

BEM   World Council of Churches, *Baptism, Eucharist and Ministry* (WCC: Geneva, 1982) (M = Ministry section)

DS   Denzinger-Schönmetzer. *Enchiridion Symbolorum* 33rd ed. (Freiburg: Herder, 1965).

WA   *D. Martin Luthers Werke, Kritische Gesamtausgabe.* The Weimar Edition (1883 ff.). References give the volume, page, and line number.

ACKNOWLEDGEMENTS

This book had its origins in two conferences I have given recently on the priesthood. Several chapters have appeared earlier as articles. Though each article has been substantially revised, I would like to acknowledge where it was first published.

Chapter 1 first appeared in the *Irish Theological Quarterly* 55 (1990) under the title "Priesthood Today: From Sacral to Ministerial Model."

Chapter 2 was published as "Priesthood and Ministry: Service and Leadership in Today's Church," in *The Priest*, 45 (September 1989).

Chapter 3, "Priesthood and Affectivity," appeared in *Chicago Studies*, 30 (November 1991).

Chapter 4, originally given as a talk on the nature of Dominican priesthood at St. Albert's College, Oakland, was published as "What Is Dominican Priesthood?" in the Dominican journal, *Spirituality Today* 42 (1990). That article has been considerably revised, to address the general issue of priesthood in apostolic religious communities. It also includes a revision of an article, "Is the Private Mass Traditional?" published in *Worship*, 64 (1990).

Much of the analysis in chapter 5 appeared under a different form in an earlier book, *Authority and Leadership in the Church: Past Directions and Future Possibilities* (Wilmington, DE: Michael Glazier, 1989), now published under the aegis of the Liturgical Press. The material has been reorganized and expanded by the inclusion of an additional dialogue.

I am grateful to the editors of these journals, and to Michael Naughton, O.S.B., Director of the Liturgical Press, for allowing me to use these earlier works.

Finally I'd like to express my appreciation to Wilkie Au, S.J. and Michael J. Buckley, S.J., who helped in the development of particular chapters, to Michael Downey who carefully reviewed the manuscript and offered many helpful suggestions, and to Carole Keese who proofed the final product. To each of them, for their interest and generous assistance I am very grateful.

Thomas P. Rausch, S.J.

INTRODUCTION

At those times when the task of being *verbi divini min-istri,* as we of the Reformed churches say, has worried and oppressed us, have we not all felt a yearning for the "rich services" (*schönen Gottesdiensten*) of Catholi-cism, and for the enviable role of the priest at the altar? ... I once heard it announced literally at a first mass, "*Le prêtre un autre Jésus Christ!*" If only we might be such too![1]

—Karl Barth

What are they saying about priesthood today? When Karl Barth, the towering figure of twentieth century Protes-tant theology, quoted the line more than sixty years ago about a priest being another Christ, he was only saying what many Catholics believed about their priests. The position of the priest within the Catholic community was secure; the priest's role was clearly understood, and it was highly val-ued. Yet much of that clarity about priesthood seemed to evaporate in the period after the Second Vatican Council. Cardinal Joseph Ratzinger acknowledged as much in his address to the international Synod of Bishops which met in Rome in October 1990 to discuss the formation of priests. According to the cardinal, the Catholic image of priesthood

1

subsequent to the Second Vatican Council had "passed into a state of crisis."[2]

While not placing all the blame on theological grounds, Ratzinger argued in his address that Catholic theology had not responded adequately to the reformation theology of the sixteenth century and to the arguments of modern biblical exegesis which in his view were still nourished by reformation presuppositions. Certainly the polemics of the sixteenth century over the nature of the pastoral office in the church have had an impact on Catholic theology. But the roots of the contemporary crisis are far more complex. Though theology has played an important role, there are other causes as well. What is clear is that in the years following the Second Vatican Council, the way the priesthood is both understood and experienced has changed in a number of ways.[3] What are some of the causes which underlie the present crisis?

Theology of Priesthood

First, the theological understanding of priesthood has changed. Modern biblical and historical studies have challenged the concept of priesthood which has been dominant in the Roman Catholic Church for almost a millennium. Today, the emphasis is <u>no longer on the "sacred power"</u> which the priest was said to possess, setting him apart from others and giving him a unique authority. Priesthood in the contemporary church is increasingly understood in terms of <u>ministry and service, not power and authority</u>. But the frequent reduction of priesthood to ministry has left a certain confusion as to what specifically constitutes the meaning of priesthood.

At the same time, as Avery Dulles has observed, the official theology of the priesthood has been enlarged considerably by the Second Vatican Council. The council moved beyond the emphasis on the sacred functions of prayer, worship, and sacrifice which had characterized Catholic theology for more than fifteen hundred years by declaring that ordination confers the threefold function of teaching, sanctifying, and governing, thus adding the royal and prophetic functions to the traditional cultic understanding of priesthood.[4]

Dulles has sketched three contemporary schools of thought in regard to priesthood. The first group, represented by Karl Rahner and Joseph Ratzinger, defines priesthood primarily in terms of the ministry of the word. The role, first of the bishop, and then of the priest, is to proclaim the word of God. Sacramental celebration and leadership are expressions of this ministry of the word. Other commentators emphasize the cultic or sacramental ministry of the priest. Otto Semmelroth and Roger Vekemans belong to this group. A third approach stresses priesthood as community leadership. Walter Kasper and Hans Urs von Balthasar in Europe and Thomas F. O'Meara and Robert Schwartz in the U.S. are among the proponents of this view.[5] But for many priests today, questions remain about their identity precisely as priests.

Expectations of the Laity

A second problem is that the expectations of the laity regarding their priests have changed dramatically. In part, these changed expectations are a result of the Second Vatican Council, and, in part, they have been elicited by priests themselves. Perhaps nothing better symbolizes the enormity of the changes in style, function, and basic understanding of priesthood that the council asked of the church's priests than the simple step of turning the altar around to face the people.

The pre-Vatican II rite highlighted the sacral and ritualistic aspect of priesthood emphasized by Catholic theology in the centuries prior to the council. Priests had been taught that all the rubrics—those little red instructions in the missal specifying each detail of the liturgy—were binding under pain of sin. The mass was a ballet of ritual gestures, and every rubric was significant, from the more than twenty-five signs of the cross or blessings made in the course of the mass and the five different kinds of bows, to the joining of thumb and forefinger after the consecration and the exact number of inches separating the hands when extended in prayer.

Though the priest's role in the pre-conciliar liturgy was highly visible and solemnized, it was also essentially anonymous, as he whispered the eucharistic prayer with his back to the congregation. His personality was subsumed into the sacred ritual action.

All that changed with the turning of the priest to face the congregation. Now he faced the people directly, head-on, exposed as never before. As the emphasis shifted from the mystery of the rite to the celebration of the gathered community, new demands were placed upon the priest which required that he truly lead them.

It is difficult for those whose experience of church is exclusively post-conciliar to appreciate how difficult this apparently simple change was for many priests. A true story is still told in our community of one Jesuit celebrating mass facing the people for the first time. By the end of the mass, he was so unsettled that instead of the usual dismissal, "Go in peace, the *mass* is ended," he dismissed his congregation with "Go in peace, the *world* is ended."

As the mass was made less mysterious, so was the aura surrounding its principal celebrant. As he emerged in all his human weakness, the authority previously conceded automatically to his office became increasingly something he had to earn, not merely in his liturgical role, but in the full range and extent of his ministry. If the sacraments were for the people, so was the priest to be. If he was to be a leader in the church, he had to first become one among the people. If he was to call others to holiness, he had to be holy himself. His task was no longer simply to offer the holy sacrifice of the mass, but to preside over a worshiping community. He was now expected to gather the people as a community, to lead them in prayer, to speak to their experience, to invite them into the celebration of Christ's mysteries. He had to become not just a priest, but a minister, a servant of God's people.

Personal Issues for Priests

Finally, there has been a significant change in the way that many priests understand themselves, their own ministry, and what is appropriate in their own personal lives. This change in the self-understanding of many priests has many causes. Partly it reflects the changed theological understanding of priesthood. Partly it is the result of the changes in seminary and religious formation programs which followed the Second Vatican Council. Partly it reflects the changing expectations the laity have of their priests.

In 1989, a document published by the U.S. Bishops' Committee on Priestly Life and Ministry acknowledged that there is "a serious and substantial morale problem among priests."[6] One problem is the growing shortage of priests. It has been estimated that about fifty percent of the parishes and mission stations in the third world lack a resident priest. The simple fact is that today a great many Catholic communities are unable to celebrate a weekly Sunday eucharist because they lack an ordained celebrant.

There has been an overall increase in vocations to the priesthood in the twelve years of John Paul II's papacy, with the total number of seminarians jumping from 62,000 to 92,000. The increase is most evident in some third world countries. But as Pope John Paul noted in his closing address to the 1990 Synod of Bishops, some places still suffer from a dramatic lack in vocations.[7] With deaths and departures from the priesthood factored in, the gap between priests and Catholic peoples both in the United States and throughout the world continues to increase. Particularly in third world countries, the number of Catholics continues to grow faster than the number of priests.[8]

The shortage is increasingly being felt in countries with a relatively large number of priests like the United States. Consider the decline in the number of diocesan seminarians in the U.S. over the last thirty years. In 1968, there were 22,334 diocesan seminarians preparing for the priesthood. In 1978 the number had dropped to 9,560. In 1988, the total number was 4,981. By 2005, it is estimated that forty-six percent of the active diocesan clergy in the U.S. will be fifty-five or older and only twelve percent thirty-four or younger.[9]

In October 1988 the U.S. Catholic bishops approved a "Directory for Sunday Celebrations in the Absence of a Priest," a rite for a lay-led communion service which could serve Catholic congregations lacking a priest for the Sunday worship.[10] But this effort at addressing the shortage of priests is not without its own problems. Many priests are forced into becoming traveling sacramental ministers, rather than resident pastors. At the same time, there is a risk of a loss of Catholic identity for communities which must celebrate a non-traditional communion service rather than a Sunday eucharist.[11]

The shortage of priests means that many good priests

today are overworked. Several years ago on retreat I met a young priest from the Philippines who had left his country in a state of near collapse. He told me that each weekend he had to celebrate at least eight masses in the rural communities surrounding Manila. Such a schedule is beyond the capabilities of even the best celebrants.

In the United States priests in parish ministry find that the demands on their time are constantly increasing. They are expected to be present at the meetings of the innumerable groups and committees in the parish. Because of the shortage of priests, some priests must take charge of a number of parishes. Many feel that the official church is unwilling to face the problem of the shortage of priests realistically. As the document on the morale of priests points out, some priests are discouraged because "some solutions to the clergy shortage are precluded from discussion and ... not all pastoral solutions and options can be explored."[12]

The cumulative effect of these new theologies of priesthood, changing expectations on the part of the laity, and new personal issues for priests themselves has been both to challenge those who have felt themselves called to the priesthood and to place new burdens upon them. To talk about priesthood today entails talking about these issues.

The 1990 Synod of Bishops, meeting in Rome on the theme "The Formation of Priests in the Circumstances of the Present Day," attempted to address some of these issues. Bishops gave papers on the theology of the priesthood, priestly identity, psychosexual development, celibacy, and various formation issues, including different types of formation, the role of women and lay people in the formation process, and lifelong formation.[13] One Synod proposition called for a "propaedeutic year" of religious formation, to be done by candidates for the priesthood before the study of philosophy and theology.[14] But no new initiatives emerged from the Synod. In his closing remarks, the pope made clear that one suggestion, to consider ordaining married men, would not be taken into consideration.[15]

In this book we will consider what is being said about the Catholic priesthood in the closing years of the twentieth century. First, we will consider the shift that has taken place in the theological understanding of the priesthood. It is important to understand how the sacral model of priesthood which dominated Catholic thinking about the priesthood from the middle ages to the end of the Second Vatican Council developed and why there has been a shift to an emphasis on ministry and leadership rather than on sacred power. We will also examine a representational model of priesthood.

We will not consider the question of the ordination of women. Though the question is important and ultimately must be faced, it is not clear that the question is really a theological one. Certainly not many people have been convinced by the arguments which have been advanced *against* the ordination of women. At the same time, more and more Catholics are becoming accustomed to and comfortable with professionally trained and competent women exercising ministerial roles which were previously reserved for priests. Many are asking why women cannot be ordained. However this question might ultimately be resolved, what does seem clear at the moment is that there will be no change in regard to the requirements for ordination in the immediate future.

The second and third chapters are more pastoral. Chapter 2 will focus on priesthood as ministry. All ministry is to be loving service of others, done in Jesus' name. But what does it mean concretely today to minister as a priest? What is it that contemporary Catholic people expect of their priests?

The third chapter is on priesthood and affectivity. It assumes that, regardless of what may happen in the future, at this moment in the life of the church celibacy will remain the rule, and addresses the challenge of living a celibate life. What is the place of affective relationships in the life of a celibate priest? How have the generationally different seminary and religious formation experiences and the different religious subcultures they represent shaped the attitudes of priests toward their own affectivity? How can priests who are called to celibacy continue to grow in the area of affectivity? Also involved in the question of affectivity is the related question of sexual identity.

The fourth chapter will note briefly different types of priesthood and focus on how priesthood should be understood in apostolic religious communities. This issue has long been neglected, though some are beginning to address it today.

In the fifth chapter we will turn to the episcopal office. According to the Second Vatican Council, the bishops are marked with the fullness of the sacrament of orders (LG 26) and possess the highest degree of the priesthood (LG 28). Thus we will consider the office and ministry of bishops, both in relation to priests and in the broader ecumenical context of the larger Christian community.

Despite the sense of many today that the ecumenical movement has been sidetracked, it remains true that a great deal has been accomplished in the now more than twenty-five years of dialogue which have followed the council. Dialogues have moved from questions of eucharist, ordained ministry, authority, and episcopacy to studies on justification, mariology, and devotion to the saints. The statements produced by these bilateral and multilateral consultations represent the closest thing to a genuinely common theology, one which is able to combine to a considerable degree the concerns and interests of the participating churches. A surprising degree of consensus has been reached.

As the dialogue progresses, one issue which continually has surfaced and has come into focus is that of the episcopal office. Episcopacy remains a difficult question. First, it concerns authority, and authority is always a difficult issue. Second, episcopacy raises the neuralgic questions of the recognition of the ministry of other churches and of apostolic succession. It also necessitates an ecumenical agreement on the nature of ordained ministry. Finally and perhaps most significantly, a consideration of episcopacy often shifts the focus in ecumenical dialogue away from a consensus on theological issues toward praxis, toward the concrete steps which can be taken on the road to reconciliation through a shared exercise of the episcopal office, and thus toward a common ordained ministry. This concern for episcopacy and ordained ministry in tomorrow's church is also part of the consideration of priesthood today.

A summary sixth chapter will attempt to gather together what we have found into some conclusions.

It is clear that the church will continue to reflect on the nature of its ordained ministry and how that ministry can be best realized in the life of the church. If the present time represents a crisis for the Catholic priesthood, it may also present the church with a *kairos*, a critical moment, a time for a new understanding and perhaps new expressions of priesthood. The priesthood is not something static; it has been open to considerable diversity in form and expression in the past and will probably be more diversely expressed in the future.

But in the meantime, there is much to be said about those who are priests today. Hopefully, this book will be a contribution toward understanding the contemporary nature of priesthood as well as the more personal issue of what it means to be a priest in today's church.

Notes

1. Karl Barth, *The Word of God and the Word of Man* (Boston: Pilgrim Press, 1928), p. 113.

2. Joseph Cardinal Ratzinger, "Biblical Foundations of Priesthood," *Origins* 20 (1990) 310.

3. See for example David N. Power, *The Christian Priest: Elder and Prophet* (London: Sheed and Ward, 1973); Robert M. Schwartz, *Servant Leaders of the People of God* (New York: Paulist Press, 1989), ch. 1, "The American Priest in Context."

4. Avery Dulles, "Models for Ministerial Priesthood," *Origins* 20 (1990) 286-287.

5. Ibid. p. 287.

6. "Reflections on the Morale of Priests," *Origins* 18 (January 12, 1989) 499.

7. Pope John Paul II, "Closing Address to the Synod," *Origins* 20 (1990) 379.

8. See Dean Hoge, *Future of Catholic Leadership: Response to the Priest Shortage* (Kansas City: Sheed & Ward, 1987), p. 5.

9. "Study of U.S. Diocesan Priesthood Statistics: 1966–2005," (Schoenherr Report) *Origins* 20 (1990) 206.

10. *Origins* 18 (1988) 301-307.

11. Cf. Rembert Weakland, "Future Parishes and the Priesthood Shortage," *Origins* 20 (1991) 539. See also the report of the National Federation of Priests' Councils, "Priestless Parishes: Priests' Perspectives," *Origins* 21 (1991) 41-53.

12. "Reflections on the Morale of Priests," p. 500.

13. The papers can be found in *Origins* 20 (October 18–November 15, 1990).

14. Synod 1990, "Overview of Proposals," *Origins* 20 (1990) 354.

15. Pope John Paul II, "Closing Address," p. 378.

1. PRIESTHOOD TODAY: THREE MODELS

Some ten years after the close of the Second Vatican Council, in a perceptive article entitled "What Went Wrong?" the American church historian and commentator Martin Marty pointed to the council's failure to provide a new rationale for what he called the church's "service ranks," its priests and religious, as constituting a major problem. The council, he argued, gave new morale to the episcopacy in its treatment of the episcopal office. And it had a great deal to say about what it meant to be a lay person in the church. "But," he wrote, "no fresh rationales for being a priest or a religious emerged, while the old ones were effectively undercut by the advances in understanding of bishop and lay person."[1]

The problem in regard to the priesthood involves more than an increased emphasis on the laity and the episcopacy. Essentially part of the crisis of the ordained ministry for Roman Catholics is the fact that the one concept which has traditionally characterized the vocation and role of the ordained minister in the Catholic tradition has itself been called into question, namely, the concept of a special, "sacral" priesthood. This concept understands the priest as a sacred person, set apart by ordination, and in possession of special sacramental power. Often described as "another Christ" (*alter Christus*), the priest was seen as a mediator between God and God's people.

The period after the council saw a general rejection of the sacral view of priesthood. No one did this more explicitly than Hans Küng: "From a New Testament point of view ... the term 'priest' should be dropped as a specific and exclusive term to identify people who have ministries in the Church, since according to the New Testament view, all believers are 'priests.'"[2]

On the other hand, Avery Dulles cautioned against rejecting too quickly the sacral dimension of the ordained ministry:

> In Roman Catholicism today we are witnessing a full-scale revolt against the excesses of the sacral concept of ministry. Rejection of this stereotype is one of the sources of the present crisis in the Church. Still there are valid elements in this controverted view.... As a focal center for the community the priest must visibly be a sign and sacrament of Christ. Catholicism has perhaps a special responsibility to keep alive this sacral dimension.[3]

Dulles of course is correct in pointing to the rejection of a sacral concept of ordained ministry as being one of the central issues in the present discussion about priesthood. Theologically, most contemporary Roman Catholic treatments of ordained ministry stress the differences between the more traditional sacral model and a more contemporary model which understands priesthood as a ministry of leadership in the ecclesial community.[4] On a practical level, in many theological centers today, where lay men and

women study for ministry with those preparing for ordination, the word priesthood itself is rarely heard; it is at least
tacitly banned and sometimes specifically rejected, lest
those who cannot or choose not to be ordained feel slight-
ed. The result is not infrequently a loss of identity for those
preparing to be priests.

What can be said about priesthood today? In addition
to the sacral and ministerial models of priesthood, Dulles has
recently proposed what he calls a "representational" model
of priesthood.[5] In this chapter, we will consider the history of
these three models, as well as their strengths and weaknesses.

The Sacral Model

Though its roots lie in a number of developments centuries earlier, the sacral model of priesthood dominated the
Roman Catholic understanding of ordained ministry in the
period from the twelfth century down to the Second Vatican Council. A review of the development of this model
brings into focus its problematic character. The sacral concept of priesthood is not evident from the New Testament;
it reflects a medieval sacralization of the priest's office, and
it implies an inadequate concept of sacramental power.

1. New Testament Evidence

The New Testament evidence is complicated, and can
be argued in either a Catholic or a Protestant direction. On
the one hand, the New Testament does not speak of Christian ministers (called apostles, prophets, teachers, presbyters, bishops, etc.) as priests. It speaks of Jewish priests, it
identifies Jesus as high priest (Hebrews), and it refers to the
entire community as a "royal priesthood" (1 Pet. 2:9). But
the word priest (*hiereus/sacerdos*) is never used in the New

Testament of ordained ministers. At the time of the reformation Luther used 1 Peter (and Revelation 5:10) to argue that all Christians were priests in virtue of their baptism, and hence that there was no need of a cultic priesthood different in kind from that of all believers.[6]

Perhaps the closest the New Testament comes to a sacral description of church ministry occurs in Romans 15:16, where Paul speaks of his own ministry of bringing the gospel to the Gentiles in language taken from the Jewish cult or liturgy. He writes that God has given him the grace to be a "cultic minister" (*leitourgon*) of Christ "in performing the priestly service (*hierourgounta*) of the gospel of God, so that the offering up (*prosphora*) of the Gentiles may be acceptable, sanctified by the Holy Spirit." Thus Paul is comparing his own missionary work to that of Jewish priests in the temple. In a similar way, 1 Peter 2 speaks of the entire Christian community as a "holy priesthood" offering "spiritual sacrifices" (v. 5) or a "royal priesthood" (*basileion hierateuma*) (v. 9). But there is nothing in the New Testament to suggest the presence of a special ministry of priests, as opposed to a non-priestly laity.

If the New Testament does not apply the language of priesthood to its official leaders, the titles "priest" and "high priest" begin to appear in patristic sources (Tertullian, Hippolytus) early in the third century, applied to the ministry of the bishops. Küng attributes this to a "less careful" use of language.[7] However Küng's own theology resembles that of the radical Hellenists in the New Testament period, a particular group who were unable to see any continuing significance in the Jewish cult. As Raymond Brown has shown, the radical Hellenists, represented by the replacement theology of Hebrews and the gospel of John, saw Jewish cult, sacrifice, temple, and priesthood as superseded, replaced by the person and work of Christ.[8]

But this replacement theology, favored by Küng and others, is only one particular New Testament tradition. According to Brown, other, more conservative early Christians, such as the Jewish Christians and their converts associated with James and Peter, remained more appreciative of the Jewish tradition, particularly its cultic language. This was true of the church of Rome, a church most probably established by Christians from this group.[9] We have already noted Paul's usage of language taken from the Jewish cult in his letter to that church.

It is interesting to note that in spite of the polemic in Hebrews against a renewed interest in the levitical cult, a letter considered by Brown and others to have been addressed to the church of Rome, that church continued to find some Jewish cultic language appropriate.[10] Thus there were some New Testament traditions which were more open to cultic language and imagery and which would ultimately use cultic language of their ministerial leaders.

In 1 Clement, written from Rome about the year 96, the author compares the order of the Jewish cult with its high priests, priests, and levites in chapter 40 with the order of the Christian community, with its apostles, bishops and deacons, in chapter 42. He also speaks of offering sacrifices as one of the roles of the episcopate (44:4). Not long afterward, other Roman church leaders began referring to the bishops in the language of priesthood. In the ordination of a bishop, the prayer of consecration which comes to us from Hippolytus of Rome (c. 220) refers to the bishop as "high priest" (*Apostolic Tradition* 3, 4). Soon other churches were referring, first to bishops, and then to presbyters as priests. The deacons, who assisted the bishop and shared in the *diakonia* of building up the community, were not described as "priests" (*Apost. Trad.* 9, 2).

2. Sacralization

In the period between the fourth and the tenth centuries, the pastoral office underwent a process of sacralization and clericalization which had the effect of erecting barriers between the priest and the people. In the decades following the Edict of Milan (313) which legitimated the church's position within the Roman empire, first bishops and then priests began to take on the privileges, honors, and marks of distinction previously reserved to high imperial officials.

Schillebeeckx has called attention to a number of developments which contributed to the sacralizing of the ministry. The spread of the church into rural areas led to the emergence of "country priests" whose primary function was to preside at local liturgies. The beginning of the practice of private celebrations of the eucharist, the increasing emphasis on abstinence from sexual intercourse prior to celebrating the eucharist, and, ultimately, the law of celibacy also tended to emphasize the relation between the priest and the eucharist rather than between the priest and the community.[11]

Even the language of the priest set him off, as Latin ceased being the common language of the people, but remained the language of liturgy. The language barrier which resulted greatly encouraged the notion of a priestly office with distinctive sacred duties.[12] The priest was coming to be understood more and more as a sacred person.

3. Sacramental Power

A third problem with the sacral model is that it implies an inadequate concept of sacramental power. In his recent study of the ordained ministry, Kenan Osborne sees an early step toward what became the scholastic concept of priesthood as a spiritual power in the writings of John Chrysostom (d. 407). In his very influential book on the priesthood (*Peri Hierosyne*), Chrysostom made popular the concept of the priest as mediator.[13]

Osborne calls attention to a number of factors which contributed to a theological emphasis on the priest rather than on the bishop. As a result of this shift of focus, scholastic theologians from 1100 defined holy orders, not in terms of the bishop, but in terms of the priest who provided the eucharist. The increasingly rural situation of the church in the Frankish or Carolingian kingdoms and the fact that local priests were often appointed by lay or religious proprietors meant that there were few ties between rural churches and the urban cathedral. The priest became the primary minister of the local community and his principal role was the celebration of the eucharist. The growing power of the pope at the cost of the collegial role of the episcopacy was another factor in the emergence of a view of priesthood based on sacramental power. The bishop's superiority came to be understood as jurisdictional, rather than sacramental, with his authority coming from the pope.[14]

The development of canon law also contributed to an understanding of priesthood in terms of sacramental power. In the eleventh and twelfth centuries canonists began to distinguish between the power of ordination and the power of jurisdiction. This in turn led to an emphasis on the "sacred power" (*sacra potestas*) of the priest, quite apart from his relation to a particular community.[15]

Medieval theology focused on this concept of spiritual or sacramental power in its approach to ordination and priesthood. In Peter Lombard, who apparently offered the first definition of the sacrament of orders, the word "spiritual power" was specifically linked with order.[16] In the work of Thomas Aquinas, the power given by orders was also linked with eucharist. Though Thomas was not the first to make this connection, his work became normative for the manualists who followed him:

> Now the power of orders is established for the dispensation of the sacraments... [and] is principally ordered to consecrating the body of Christ and dispensing it to the faithful, and to cleansing the faithful from their sins.[17]

It is interesting to note that Aquinas does not mention preaching among the responsibilities of the priest.

Liturgical development also played a role. The ordination rite of the western church was complicated by the accretion over the centuries of various liturgical traditions in addition to the prayer of consecration and the laying-on of hands. The practice of "handing over of the instruments" (*traditio instrumentorum*) arose in the Gallican churches and was included in the *Romano-Germanic Pontifical* of Mainz (950); from there it reached Rome where it was incorporated into the Roman ordination ritual. Along with this development went an increasing emphasis on the power to offer sacrifice. The general Council of Florence in the Decree for the Armenians (1439), following the opinion of Aquinas, taught that the matter for ordination to the priesthood was the handing over of the chalice with the wine and the paten with the bread, and the form, citing the *Pontificale Romanum,* the words "receive the power of offering sacrifice in the Church for the living and the dead" (DS 1326). Pope Pius XII in the Apostolic Constitution *Sacramentum Ordinis* (30 November 1947) clarified the matter and form of the sacrament of orders, stating that "at least in the future the handing over of the instruments is not necessary for the validity of the holy orders of diaconate, priesthood and episcopate" (DS 3859).

Thus medieval theology along with certain developments in the liturgy provided the theological rationale for the sacral view of the priesthood by stressing the concept of sacramental power. This view was confirmed by the Council of Trent in its canons on the sacrament of orders:

> If anyone shall say that there is not in the New Testament a visible and external priesthood, or that there is no power of consecrating and offering the true body and blood of the Lord and of forgiving and retaining sins, but only the office and bare ministry of preaching the Gospel; or that those who do not preach are not priests at all—*anathema sit* (DS 1771).

In post-reformation Roman Catholic textbook theology this emphasis on sacramental power led to what has been unhappily but accurately called a "theology of confection."[18] The priest was equipped with sacramental power to "confect" the eucharist. This theology was characteristic of Roman Catholic theology of priesthood until the Second Vatican Council.

4. Evaluation

There are a number of strengths to the sacral model of priesthood. An emphasis on the ordained ministry as priesthood has helped to express the eucharistic orientation of the church's ministry of leadership as well as the nature of the church itself as a eucharistic community. It has also contributed to a "high sacerdotal spirituality"[19] which has attracted many to the priesthood, and provided them with a strong sense of identity. The sacral model of priesthood has considerable support in official church teaching from the time of the Council of Florence (1439). Some consider it simply a case of doctrinal development.

But there are also some decided disadvantages to the

sacral model. The New Testament does not describe ordained ministers as priests, and it does not attribute to them
special powers not shared by the rest of the community. In
stressing the priest's cultic role at the expense of the concept of ministry, it reduces priesthood to eucharistic presidency and can lead to a false view of the priest as a person
possessed of special powers. Sacramentality can be easily
misunderstood as type of magic. Thus a sacral model of
priesthood can be easily misinterpreted. The sacral model
also tends to separate the priest from the community, a sep-
aration reinforced by obligatory celibacy, special privileges,
and clerical dress. Finally, its elitism is very much out of
synch with the contemporary sense of the church as a community of disciples or even as an egalitarian community.

The Ministerial Model

Since the Second Vatican Council, Roman Catholic
theology has stressed a ministerial model of priesthood.[20]
Priesthood as a ministry of community leadership is not
really a new idea; it has always been presupposed, though
its obvious meaning has frequently been lost sight of and
covered over in the sacralizing of the priesthood and the
clericalizing of its order which took place over so many centuries. We spoke of priests as "sacred ministers," but the
emphasis was always on the word sacred, not on minister.

Whence comes this concept of priesthood as a ministry or service of community leadership? Here it might be
helpful to review *diakonia*, community leadership, and
eucharistic presidency in the New Testament.

1. Diakonia

Though the early Christians had available a number of
terms designating those who exercised leadership and

authority in the community, including the word "priest" (*hiereus*),[21] they chose the Greek word *diakonos*, servant, from *diakonein* and its cognate, *diakonia*. Modern scholars, largely on the basis of H. W. Beyer's article in Kittel's *Theological Dictionary of the New Testament*, have understood *diakonein* as being originally a secular term for service; specifically the verb *diakonein* meant to serve at table. The *diakonos* was the one who served at table, a servant.

The function of the *diakonos* was not a prestigious one. As Hans Küng has said, "The distinction between master and servant was nowhere more visually apparent than at meals, where the noble masters would lie at the table in their long robes, while the servants, their clothes girded, had to wait on them."[22] Thus Küng and other scholars have argued that when the early Christians wanted to identify those who exercised roles of leadership in the community, they chose words which in their original context meant service at table.

However, a recent investigation of the meaning of *diakonia* and its cognates in the original Greek sources has challenged this traditional understanding of the term. In his book, *Diakonia: Re-interpreting the Ancient Sources*, John Collins argues that *diakonia*/ministry comes not from profane life but from religious and formal language, with implications of authorization or divine representation.[23] An important implication for Collins from this analysis is that ministry is not for all the baptized; it is based on the word and restricted (not necessarily to males or celibates) to those to whom it has been given by the community or by the Lord.[24] Collins' work has yet to be carefully evaluated, but it certainly will be controversial.

Was there a connection between the concept of leadership and authority as *diakonia*/service (whether authorized or not) and Jesus himself? The answer clearly is yes.

The gospels depict Jesus as describing his own life and role in terms of serving others (Mk 10:45; Lk 22:27; John 13:1-20), and recent studies argue that these traditions are rooted in the historical Jesus.[25]

2. Leadership

The word *diakonia* first appears in the New Testament in the letters of St. Paul. Paul makes it clear that there is a diversity of gifts (*charismata*) and ministries (*diakonoi*) (1 Cor 12:4-5), service gifts and roles given for the common good (1 Cor 12:7), for the building up of the church (1 Cor 14:5, 12). He sometimes uses *diakonia* in the more general sense of service, in reference to his efforts to support financially the Jerusalem church (Rom 15:25, 31; 2 Cor 8:4, 19; 9:1) and for personal service (Phlm 13).

But most often he uses *diakonia* and *diakonos* of those whose particular form of Christian service places them in leadership roles in the community. Thus in his letters *diakonia* or its substantive is used in connection with Paul's own apostolic ministry (Rom 1:1; 15:16; 1 Cor 4:1; 2 Cor 3:6; 6:4; 11:8; 11:23), or in reference to others claiming to be apostles (2 Cor 11:12, 15), or of local community ministers (Rom 16:1; Phil 1:1), among them Phoebe of the church of Cenchreae (Rom 16:1), a woman.

Already within the New Testament period, this ministry of community leadership was recognized as an office, linked to the ministry of the apostles (Acts 14:23; 1 Tim 5:22; 1 Pet 5:1). The one who presides over the local community and its worship today must remain linked to the original apostolic ministry and to the wider church. This is the meaning of apostolic succession in the ordained ministry. In this way the continuity in the tradition and with the communion of the church catholic is expressed.

3. Eucharistic Presidency

Who presided at the eucharist in the primitive church? The New Testament does not provide a clear answer to this question. From parallels with Jewish practice, it has been suggested that the heads of the "house churches" (Rom 16:5; 1 Cor 16:19; Col 4:15) or hosts led the communities gathered in their homes, proclaiming the word and perhaps presiding at the eucharist. But this remains a suggestion; it cannot be proved.

The prophets and teachers are thought to have included presiding at the eucharist among their roles. In Paul's churches they seem to have been local leaders; in 1 Corinthians 12:28 he lists them in a position of prominence, right after the apostles. In Acts 13:2 the prophets and teachers at Antioch are described as "engaged in the liturgy (*leitourgountōn*) of the Lord." The *Didache* recognizes prophets and teachers as eucharistic leaders (10:7), though it urges the election of bishops and deacons, pointing out that "they too conduct the liturgy of the prophets and teachers" (15:1).

The laying on of hands emerged within the New Testament period as the sign of appointment to the office of church leader. But the first explicit linking of the eucharist with church leaders comes with Ignatius of Antioch (c. 115): "You should regard that Eucharist as valid which is celebrated either by the bishop or by someone he authorizes" (Symrneans 8:1). Thus presiding over the community also meant presiding over its eucharist; it was not the other way around. In fact, as Hervé-Marie Legrand has argued, the modern problem of a community unable to celebrate the eucharist would not have arisen. The community would always choose a local leader who would then be appointed with the help of the heads of neighboring churches.[26]

4. Evaluation

Our review of ministry, leadership, and eucharistic presidency has shown several important relationships. First, the New Testament concept of ministry, *diakonia*, is rooted in Jesus himself who took the role of a servant. In the words of an early Christian hymn, he took the form of a slave and became "obedient to death, even death on a cross" (Phil 2:7-8).

Second, though Paul sometimes uses *diakonia* in a more general sense of service, he uses it most often of those in leadership roles in the church. This would be supported by the recent research of John Collins, and his argument that in Paul *diakonos* refers to authorized representatives.[27]

Third, the ministry of local community leaders came to include presiding at the eucharist. Though this ministry was not seen as explicitly sacerdotal until the early third century, the ministry of those who in the Catholic tradition are called priests should include both service and presiding at the eucharist.

There is much to recommend a ministerial or leadership model of priesthood. First, understanding priesthood within the broader category of ministry (*diakonia*) and leadership is rooted in the rediscovery of the multiplicity of charisms and ministries which characterized the primitive church, evident in 1 Corinthians 12–14 and Romans 12:4-8. The Christian community is equipped with a diversity of gifts, of leadership and administration, of preaching and teaching, of helping and healing, of conjugal love and single service.

Second, an emphasis on leadership within the community accords much better with the historical evidence of ordained ministry in the early centuries. As opposed to a sacral model which stressed the link between the priest and the eucharist, a leadership model permits a recovery of the inseparable link evident in the early centuries between the community and its leader. The modern situation of a Christian community unable to celebrate the eucharist for want of a priest would have been unthinkable.

Third, an emphasis on priesthood as ministry speaks to the experience of many contemporary Roman Catholics who are claiming their own participation in the church's ministry. In many ways Vatican II reclaimed for lay people a share in the mission of the church. Though the Dogmatic Constitution on the Church, *Lumen Gentium,* said that the hierarchical priesthood and the common priesthood "differ from one another in essence and not only in degree," it raised this point to teach that both priesthoods participate in the one priesthood of Christ (LG 10). The council stressed that the laity also share in the priestly, prophetic, and kingly functions of Christ (LG 31) and participate in the mission of the church itself (LG 33). The council did not go so far as to speak of ministries ordained and non-ordained, but its stress on a diversity of gifts, "both hierarchical and charismatic" (LG 4), was clearly a move in that direction.

The concept of the priest as a sacred person, different from the baptized, is not a congenial one to many Catholics today who understand the church as the people of God, a community of disciples, even an egalitarian community.[28] These men and women are deeply dedicated to the church and want to claim their own ministries within it. Though they welcome priests as colleagues and friends, they no longer accord them authority and respect automatically. Neither can be taken for granted.

There are also some disadvantages to a description of priesthood simply in terms of a ministry of leadership. First, an overemphasis on ordained ministry as community leadership does not address the situation of religious priests who in most cases do not exercise their priesthood by presiding over stable local communities. It can also slight or neglect other leadership charisms within the community. Scholars, educators, pastoral leaders, those with prophetic insight and those who witness on behalf of justice also exercise leadership roles in the church.

Second, the desacralization of the priesthood has led to a loss of identity for many priests. If ministry or service becomes the basic category, it becomes difficult to say what is specific to ordained ministry. As Roger Mahony, archbishop (now cardinal) of Los Angeles has emphasized, within such a functional theology, priesthood becomes more of a job than a special call. A great emphasis is placed on the development of the skills necessary for effective ministry, but a functional approach cannot account for the importance of a lifelong commitment, a celibate lifestyle, holiness, and a simple way of life.[29]

The passing of the sacral model has left a void; there is a need to replace the "high sacerdotal spirituality" of the past with a spirituality which can address the priesthood both in its relation to the other ministries and in its own specific identity. The recent document, "Reflections on the Morale of Priests," produced by the U.S. Bishops' Committee on Priestly Life and Ministry, calls for the development of "a spirituality truly appropriate for the parish priest. The move is away from an exclusively monastic or choir stall spirituality toward an ecclesial or ministry-centered one that does not fail to integrate the values of the past."[30]

Finally, a failure to articulate adequately the uniqueness of the priesthood, along with recent efforts to construct an egalitarian ecclesiology, has led some to suggest that ordained ministry itself is superfluous. Some have proposed a charismatic "ordination of the Spirit" as opposed to a traditional ordination by the institutional church.[31]

Sandra Schneiders, noting that non-ordained ministers often lead people to sacramental occasions for reconciliation, eucharist, and the anointing of the sick, raises the question of whether an ordained minister is always necessary to celebrate them.[32] Other women go further and ask if ordination in the traditional sense is necessary at all.[33] If priesthood is more than a ministry of leadership, its specific nature needs to be more clearly articulated and expressed.

The Representational Model

Recently Avery Dulles and others have proposed a "representational" model of priesthood. According to Dulles, the church as the body of Christ represents and makes Christ present to the world. "But for the church to be a social and public reality in the world it is also necessary for Christ to be represented by the official actions of the church as such."[34] This representational role is carried out by bishops and priests. Bishops, who possess the fullness of the priesthood, and presbyters are able to represent Christ to the church. They do so by virtue of their ordination, recognized as a sacrament or outward sign, which authorizes them to speak and act in his name. Thus by their ordination they become "ecclesiastical persons...public persons in the church."[35]

Dulles' model finds its biblical foundation in Paul's own self-understanding of the apostles as "qualified ministers of a new covenant" (2 Cor 3:6). Theologically, it is based on the implications of the priest's role in the celebration of the sacraments.

As Dulles proposes it, the representational model returns to a theology which sees the bishop as exercising the fullness of the priesthood, it moves beyond functionalism, and it reemphasizes the need for personal holiness.

1. Fullness of Priesthood

Rather than defining holy orders in terms of the pres-byter, as was the case with Catholic theology from the middle ages all the way up to Vatican II, the representational model as Dulles presents it follows *Lumen Gentium* in ascribing the fullness of the priesthood to the bishop. *Lumen Gentium* 21 speaks of the bishop as receiving the fullness of the sacrament of orders (cf. LG 26, 28). The preliminary note to *The Roman Pontifical*, revised by the council, speaks of presbyters as "priests of the second order":

> The Latin liturgical text distinguishes with the greatest care between *sacerdotium* and *presbyteratus*, *sacerdos* and *presbyter*, in accordance with tradition and with the conciliar documents, especially *Lumen gentium* and *Presbyterorum ordinis* of the Second Vatican Council. In reference to the ordained and ministerial priesthood, *sacerdos* and *sacerdotium* are used of both *episcopi* and *presbyteri*; when only the *sacerdotes* of the second order are meant, *presbyter* is used exclusively and consistently.

> This translation reflects this distinction faithfully and literally, even though it has required the used of the less common word, "presbyter," referring to priests of the second order. Only in this way was it possible to make clear the tradition which has been maintained in the revision of the ordination rites.[36]

In the rite of ordination to the presbyterate, the prayer of consecration asks that the ordinand might receive "the dignity of the order of presbyters...the second order of the hierarchy."[37] In respect to the relationship of priest to bishop, both Vatican II and the representational model are more faithful to the understanding of priesthood and orders in the ancient tradition.

2. Beyond Functionalism

Dulles sees this model as going beyond the functionalism of much contemporary theology of the ordained ministry to an ontology of priesthood. But it does so without turning the priest once more into a sacred person. His approach is careful and nuanced. He does not say that a priest is configured to Christ by ordination, as does the document on the ministerial priesthood which followed the Third Synod of Bishops (1971).[38] The Synod document here is following *Presbyterorum Ordinis,* the decree of the Second Vatican Council on the ministry of priests, which is more specific. The council's decree states that priests are "configured" to Christ by ordination so that they can "act in the person of Christ" (PO 2). This is not to suggest that the priest replaces Christ; the function is representational.

However ordination does bring about a real (ontological) change in regard to the priest. By being "ordered" or ordained into the order of presbyters, a person is incorporated into the church's pastoral office. As a result, the priest has been authorized to act officially in the name of the church, and thus in Christ's name. Dulles makes it clear that bishops and priests act in Christ's name and represent him particularly in "strictly sacramental ministry and in teaching guaranteed by infallibility."[39]

Once a person has been incorporated into an order, a new relation exists between the church and the one ordained. Should the priest leave the ministry and then resume it, there is no need to repeat ordination. In the tradition of the church, "both the permanence of the priesthood and its impact on the very being of the ordained" is expressed by the notion of the "indelible character" received through ordination.[40]

3. Personal Holiness

Finally, by making it clear that the conformity to Christ is not "automatic" in those non-sacramental moments of the priest's official ministry, Dulles' approach stresses an existential dimension to priesthood which places a new importance on prayer and personal holiness.

According to Dulles, it cannot be assumed that the priest is automatically acting for Christ in those other ministerial functions, many of which are also performed by laypersons. Because priesthood is a permanent vocation which makes the priest a public person in the church, the priest must strive to represent Christ by a complete and total commitment to the vocation of the priest: "To be transparent to Christ, as his vocation requires, he must prayerfully live up to his vocation and frequently 'rekindle the gift of God' that is in him through the laying on of hands (cf. 2 Tm 1:6)."[41] Holiness of life is important. Thus the training of priests requires spiritual formation as well as practical and theological education.

4. Evaluation

There are a number of advantages to Dulles' representational model. Understanding the priest's role as representational, as one who has been authorized by the church to act in Christ's name, helps to bring into focus the unique and specific aspect of the priesthood. The priest is not the only leader in the Christian community, but the priest does represent Christ in the official actions of the church.

Unlike the ministry as community leadership model, the representational model describes a priesthood appropriate to both diocesan and religious priests who generally are not pastors of local parish communities.

Some may object that the model returns to a sacral

understanding of the priest. It is true that early on Dulles recognized "valid elements" in the sacral concept.[42] But the representational model is different from a sacral model in significant ways. As Rahner has argued, the concept of sacramental power is not an adequate starting point for a definition of priestly ministry today.[43] The representational model is grounded on the priest's role in the celebration of the sacraments, not on a concept of sacramental power. It does not represent a metaphysical clericalism, placing the priest on a higher level of being than the others in the church. The priest is not a sacred person, is not understood as an exclusive mediator between God and God's people, and does not personally exercise all ministerial functions in the church. Ministry in the church is not limited to the ordained, and any Christian ministering to another in the Spirit can mediate an experience of God's forgiveness, healing, and love.

But as one who has been sacramentally authorized, the priest becomes one able to act in the name of the church and thus in the place of Christ. This does give a special significance, an ecclesial character even to the non-sacramental dimensions of the priest's ministry.

Catholicism's traditional emphasis on the unique character of sacramental causality does not restrict or limit grace to the structure of the sacraments themselves. Nor does Catholicism deny that graced moments outside of this structure may communicate the grace of the sacraments (the *res sacramenti*).[44] Grace transcends the sacraments.

But the church does recognize that grace is present in its sacraments. It is able to affirm the presence of grace in the case of those sacramental moments presided over by the priest who has been sacramentally authorized to act in its name. The church does not recognize as valid sacraments (excluding baptism) administered by those who have not been sacramentally authorized.

Conclusions

The word "priest" (*prêtre, prete, presbitero, Priester*) is derived etymologically from the Greek word *presbyteros* which originally meant "an older man" or "elder." In the New Testament *presbyteros* is usually employed as a technical term for a church official or leader. The term was borrowed from Jewish nomenclature, though in neither its Jewish nor in its Christian sense did it mean "priest" in the cultic sense of the *hiereus/sacerdos*. However the English word priest carries both connotations.

The cultic terms *hiereus/sacerdos*, used first of the bishop, began to appear early in the third century as the church came to recognize the sacrificial dimensions of its eucharist, a recognition already present in the *Didache* (14) at least a century earlier. The language of priesthood is deeply rooted in the tradition of the church. It has served to underline the eucharistic orientation of the church's ministry of leadership and of the church itself; the church is not just a community, it is a eucharistic community. Even if the sacral model does not adequately describe the ordained ministry, there is no reason to exclude the language of priesthood, or to reduce priesthood simply to ministry, thus suggesting that there is not something unique or specific to the ministry of the ordained.

The sacral concept of priesthood developed out of the ordained minister's presidential role in the worship or cult of the community. The celebration of the eucharist remains central to the office of the priest. But in terms of the way that ordained ministry is understood theologically, it seems clear that a sacral model of priesthood will be even less adequate for an understanding of ordained ministry in the future.

More sensitive to the multiplicity of charisms and ministries which characterized the New Testament church, recent theology has described priesthood in terms of ministry and leadership. Priesthood means a ministry of leadership—or perhaps better, of servant leadership—in word, sacrament, and the life of the community of faith. The ministerial model has good roots historically and it is able to speak to a number of contemporary concerns. But this model too has limitations.

The representational model seeks to address what is specific to the ministry of the priest. Through ordination, the priest is authorized to speak in the name of the church, and in certain cases to act in Christ's name. Aside from these sacramental moments, a priest must strive to live out the vocation of priesthood fully, if Christ is to be transparent within the priest's ministry. In other words, the priest is not a sacred person. But precisely because priests are public persons in the church, authorized to speak in its name, people expect them to represent Christ.

Though not all priesthood is expressed in leading stable local communities, the church today desperately needs priests who can form and lead such communities of faith.

Notes

1. Martin Marty, "What Went Wrong?" *The Critic* 34 (Fall 1975) 53.

2. Hans Küng, *Why Priests? A Proposal for a New Church Ministry* (Garden City, NY: Doubleday, 1974), p. 42.

3. Avery Dulles, *Models of the Church* (Garden City, NY: Doubleday, 1974), pp. 158-159.

4. For example, Küng, *Why Priests?*; Edward Schillebeeckx *Ministry: Leadership in the Community of Jesus Christ* (New York: Crossroad, 1981).

5. Avery Dulles, "Models for Ministerial Priesthood," *Origins* 20 (1990) 288.

6. WA 6.407. 22-25; 6.564. 6-13.

7. Küng, *Why Priests?* p. 54.

8. Raymond E. Brown and John P. Meier, *Antioch & Rome* (New York: Paulist Press, 1983), pp. 6-8.

9. Ibid. pp. 110-122.

10. Ibid. pp. 154-155.

11. See Schillebeeckx, *Ministry*, pp. 48-58; *The Church with a Human Face* (New York: Crossroad, 1985), pp. 141–151.

12. David N. Power, "Evolution of the Priesthood,"' *Church* 16 (Fall 1988) 17.

13. Kenan B. Osborne, *Priesthood: A History of the Ordained Ministry in the Roman Catholic Church* (New York: Paulist Press, 1988), pp. 148–155.

14. Ibid. pp. 169-190.

15. See Schillebeeckx, *Church with a Human Face*, pp. 192-193.

16. Osborne, *Priesthood*, pp. 204-205.

17. Thomas Aquinas, *Summa Contra Gentiles*, Bk. 4, chap. 74, 75 (New York: Image Books, 1957), pp. 287, 289.

18. Joseph M. Powers, "Eucharist: Symbol of Freedom and Community," in Francis A. Eigo and Silvio E. Fittipaldi (ed.), *Christian Spirituality in the United States: Independence and Interdependence* (Philadelphia: Villanova University Press, 1978), pp. 187-197.

19. Cf. Avery Dulles, *Models of the Church*, p. 158. For an exaggerated example of such a spirituality see Fulton Sheen, *The Priest Is Not His Own* (New York: McGraw-Hill, 1963).

20. See for example Robert M. Schwartz, *Servant Leaders of the People of God* (New York: Paulist Press, 1989).

21. See Yves Congar, *Power and Poverty in the Church* (Baltimore: Helicon, 1965), pp. 37-38; Hans Küng, *The Church* (New York: Sheed and Ward, 1967), pp. 388–390.

22. Hans Küng, *The Church*, p. 390.

23. John N. Collins, *Diakonia: Re-interpreting the Ancient Sources* (New York: Oxford University Press, 1990).

24. Ibid. pp. 258-259.

25. See Walter Kasper, *Jesus the Christ* (New York: Paulist Press, 1976), pp. 120-121; Edward Schillebeeckx, *Jesus* (New York: Crossroad, 1981), p. 311.

26. See Hervé-Marie Legrand, "The Presidency of the Eucharist According to the Ancient Tradition," *Worship* 53 (1979) 437.

27. Collins, *Diakonia*, pp. 195–212.

28. Cf. Sandra M. Schneiders, "Evangelical Equality," *Spirituality Today* 38 (1986) 293-302.

29. Roger Mahony, "A Focus for Priestly Ministry: A Pastoral Letter to Priests," *Origins* 15 (1986) 640.

30. "Reflections on the Morale of Priests," *Origins* 18 (1989) 502.

31. John W. Glaser, "Anonymous Priesthood," *Commonweal* 93 (11 December 1970) 271-274.

32. Sandra M. Schneiders, "Ministry and Ordination, I," *The Way* 20 (1980) 296.

33. Cf. Letty Russell, "Unity and Renewal in Feminist Perspec-

tive," *Ecumenical Trends* 16 (1987) 190; Una M. Kroll, "Beyond the Ordination Issue," *The Ecumenical Review* 40 (1985) 57-65.

34. Dulles, "Models for Ministerial Priesthood," p. 288. Archbishop Daniel Pilarczyk developed a similar approach at the 1990 Synod of Bishops on "The Formation of Priests in the Circumstances of the Present Day" in a talk entitled "Defining the Priesthood," published in *Origins* 20 (1990) 297-300.

35. Ibid.

36. *The Roman Pontifical*, Revised by Decree of the Second Vatican Council, Preliminary Note (Toronto: International Committee on English in the Liturgy, 1970).

37. Ibid. p. 4.

38. Synod of Bishops, *The Ministerial Priesthood and Justice in the World* (Washington: USCC, 1971), I, 5, 1.

39. Dulles, "Models of Ministerial Priesthood," p. 288.

40. Ibid.

41. Ibid.

42. Dulles, *Models of the Church*, p. 158.

43. Karl Rahner, "What Is the Theological Starting Point for a Definition of the Priestly Ministry?" in *The Identity of the Priest*, ed. Karl Rahner, Concilium Vol. 43 (Glen Rock, NJ: Paulist Press, 1969), p. 80.

44. Karl Rahner argues that even the *res sacramenti* of the eucharist, unity with the body of Christ, can be realized apart from the eucharist, in "Theological Reflections on the Priestly Image of Today and Tomorrow," *Theological Investigations* 12 (New York: Seabury, 1974), p. 48.

2. PRIESTHOOD AS MINISTRY

At the beginning of his fine book about a priest struggling with cancer, Paul Wilkes quotes his subject, Father Joseph Greer, warning a seminarian intern about the challenges facing someone thinking about being a priest today:

> You have to be nuts to go into the priesthood. It's an awful job. The pay is terrible, the hours are worse. People not only don't look up to you, they look down. You have to love God, and if you don't, it will grind you up. Remember, no trumpets will sound. And you're going to spend more time being a carpenter than a priest.[1]

Wilkes' book is a moving tribute to an ordinary priest who, in spite of his personal failings, strove to model his life on the example of Jesus.

The gospels depict Jesus as describing his own life and role in terms of serving others (Mk 10:45; Lk 22:27; Jn 13:1-20), and recent studies maintain that these traditions are rooted in the historical Jesus.

According to Walter Kasper, the reign of God that Jesus proclaimed took on a personal embodiment in his

own life in the form of a service of others. Jesus saw his loving service of others and ultimately his death as bringing
about a healing of human alienation and guilt. In this way
he established reconciliation or community for men and
women with God.[2] Edward Schillebeeckx writes that Jesus
faced his death "as a final and extreme service to the cause
of God as the cause of men."[3] Both authors maintain that
those gospel sayings of Jesus describing his death as a service have an historical basis in his life and intention.

This concept of service became a specifically ecclesial
concept when the primitive Christian churches adopted the
Greek word *diakonia* to express the idea of service and leadership in and for the Christian community. From *diakonia*,
through the Latin *ministerium*, we get the English word ministry. Ministry in the church must reflect that loving service
of others that Jesus modeled in his life as well as in his
death. All Christians are called to this kind of service of
others in virtue of their baptism.

But what does the concept of *diakonia*/ministry mean
today for those who are priests? We will consider three different aspects of priestly ministry in today's church: ministry as vulnerability, as reconciliation, and as leadership.

Ministry as Vulnerability

Priests are ministers, and to be a minister is, first of all,
to be called to be a servant of others, as Jesus was. To be a
servant is to be without prestige or power; it is to be always
available, at the disposal of others, to be vulnerable. A person locked behind fortress walls, whether material or psy-
chological, is not vulnerable. To be vulnerable means being
susceptible to injury, thus without defenses, open to others,
able to be affected by others. People give up their vulnerability at the cost of their humanity. Priests can afford to give

up neither. And in today's church, priests are vulnerable in a number of ways.

1. Overworked

Many priests today are overworked. As the number of priests continues to decrease, the demands on those who are active and competent continue to increase. Priests in parish ministry are not only expected to be present at the meetings of the innumerable groups and committees in the parish community, but they are also called upon for more and more special liturgies for those groups, for sub-communities in the parish, and for other groups outside the parish.

Priests living in large communities are frequently asked for liturgical service by communities of religious women. They need to be especially sensitive to these requests at this particular time in the life of the church, when many religious women are acutely aware that they are not able to provide their own celebrants because of the church's understanding of the requirements for ordination. These priests, especially when they are involved in education, have to be careful to keep a balance between privatizing their vocation as priests as they meet the professional demands that are placed upon them today and becoming overextended through taking on a liturgical/sacramental ministry that goes considerably beyond their normal responsibilities.

Not all priests of course are overworked. Some have managed to preserve for themselves a considerable part of the gracious clerical lifestyle of the past. Others fall into the "I don't do windows" syndrome, making it very clear—to the frustration of their pastors or associates—what responsibilities they are willing to take on and what tasks fall outside their particular interests. Recently one pastor told me of an associate who announced that he was not available for any calls after supper, precisely when most working people were free to see him. But most priests who approach their ministry with generosity and dedication are generally stretched too thin and are overburdened.

2. Caught in the Middle

Second, many priests today find themselves torn between a considerable number of lay people anxious for change and an official church which often seems to be more concerned with restoring discipline and recentralizing authority. As the recent document on the morale of priests prepared by the U.S. Bishops' Committee on Priestly Life and Ministry phrases it, priests are "caught in the middle."[4] Thus many priests find themselves the target of considerable frustration, and at times their ministry, if not unwelcome, is at least resented.

The alienation felt by so many contemporary women is a critical problem. Many of them have experienced condescending or patronizing attitudes on the part of individual priests; they have their own personal stories of being ignored or taken advantage of, and they resent a church in which decisions made by clerical males exclude them from full participation in ministry and priesthood. Women whose experience in the church has been painful are not infrequently resentful of the priest whose position at least seems to be based more on his gender than on his personal charism or competence.

The fact that a considerable number of deeply committed Catholic women feel a deep anger at the church which they perceive as dominated by men calls for a special sensitivity on the part of priests, even when they find themselves the target of these women's resentment. Here their own desire to imitate Jesus' example of loving service of those who have been injured will be put to the test.

Priests who dismiss the question of inclusive language as unimportant or "ideological," who are unable to work with women as equals, or who make no effort to enter into their experience need to reflect on what being a servant means practically in their lives.

The problem here is not just a male-female issue; it is also a clerical-lay issue. Today lay men as well as women, following the Second Vatican Council's stress on the importance of lay people in the church and their participation in the threefold office of Christ, are claiming their own share in the church's ministry. They resent what has sometimes been referred to as a "Pac Man" theory of ministry, which gobbles up all the important functions within the community and subsumes them within the role of the ordained. Their resentment is understandable when they feel that their own gifts cannot or will not be recognized or when they see themselves excluded from the decision-making processes of the church. For some, that resentment can easily be directed at priests who symbolize by their very presence the church's clerical structure. Others are anxious to support good priests, but they are not uncritical about those they meet.

3. Lacking Power

Finally, priests are vulnerable because they find themselves powerless to realistically address the issues that most concern themselves and those they serve. The bishops' document on the morale of priests called attention to this in several ways. It singled out a number of problems faced by priests today, among them changing or unclear role expectations, loneliness, the need for affirmation, and a number of issues related to sexuality, including psychosexual development, feminism, married clergy, optional celibacy, and the role and place of homosexuality in ministry.

The document noted that some priests experience discouragement because the solutions to the problems of the shortage of priests are "precluded from discussion."[5] In summarizing its profile of priests today it stated: "Perhaps most significant of all, [priests] feel that they have little or no control over their lives and future, be it in terms of ministry, assignment, policy development or church direction."[6]

Being overworked, caught in the middle, and lacking the power to bring about change are not assets. They represent problems which ultimately must be addressed. But they also leave the priest exposed, without defenses, vulnerable. However that vulnerability might just be an asset, if it means that the life of a priest is no longer a privileged position but a vocation which demands a commitment to discipleship and a desire to be a minister.

In the past, the priesthood at least in the United States enjoyed an enormous prestige in the Catholic community. Many of its best and brightest chose the priesthood as a vocation. For others it was a step up, a way ahead, and they responded with generosity. But today the priesthood no longer commands the same respect. The intense focus in recent years on clerical celibacy and sexuality has contributed to a diminishing respect for the priesthood and made priests themselves feel more vulnerable. So have recent scandals and revelations about pedophilic priests.

Questions have also been raised about the quality of candidates for the priesthood today. Faculty interviewed by Katarina Schuth in her study of twenty-four U.S. seminaries and theologates noted an increasing tendency toward "neoconservatism" among seminarians today. She describes these seminarians as conservative in their attitudes toward liturgy and authority, more interested in habits, vestments, and church paraphernalia, and inclined toward "the more hieratic dimensions of office and priestly roles."[7] Such candidates may be fragile psychologically, in need of a highly structured way of life. They may be drawn to the priesthood precisely because it seems to offer both status and security.

Other candidates today are reluctant to think of themselves as representing the church. They are convinced that the priesthood as it has existed in the church is in a process of transition, and they do not want to be too identified with the institution. Their view of priesthood is a highly individualistic one that risks privatizing the church's ministry of leadership.

All these problems, so widely discussed, have contributed to a loss of status for the priest's vocation today. But in the long run, this diminishment may really be a blessing in disguise. If a priest today is not automatically given the honor and respect accorded to his office in the past, if his ministry is not always recognized, if some people are inclined to look on him with suspicion simply because he is a priest, then there are significantly fewer incentives to seek the priesthood for reasons of status or personal prestige.

To be a good priest is a real challenge. It is not an easy life. It is a genuine vocation which demands the kind of commitment that can only be lived out with the help of God's grace. It is a vocation to be a leader precisely in the way that Jesus was, as one who serves. The priest is a servant of God's wounded people. The church today desperately needs this kind of servant leaders. At the same time, the church itself needs the kind of reconciliation which is so much a part of the priest's ministry.

Ministry as Reconciliation

Through his life of loving service and death, Jesus brought about a new community of men and women with God and with one another. Nowhere was the inclusive nature of that community more evident than in the practice of table fellowship which played so important a part in his public ministry. The gospels frequently show Jesus sharing meals with others. He joins Jewish officials for meals in their homes (Lk 7:36-50; 14:1-11), shares meals with his friends (Jn 2:1-11; 12:1-11; cf. Lk 10:38-42), and with sinners (Mk 2:15-17; Mt 9:10-13; Lk 15:2; 19:1-10).

In the Judaism of his day, to share a meal over which the head of the house has asked a blessing signified fellowship with God. But to break bread with those outside the law was itself an offense against the law. Jesus, however, went out of his way to make his table fellowship inclusive. "I did not come to call the righteous but sinners" (Mk 2:17). He was frequently criticized by the religious authorities for his table fellowship, for the joyful meals with his disciples (Mk 2:18-22) and for eating with outcasts: "Look, he is a glutton and a drunkard, a friend of tax collectors and sinners" (Mt 11:19). But for Jesus, sharing meals with sinners and outcasts was a sign of the inclusiveness of God's reign; no one was to be excluded from God's offer of salvation. Table fellowship was a concrete sign of forgiveness and reconciliation.

The last supper was most probably not a Passover meal, but a final gathering of Jesus and his disciples at table for one last experience of their fellowship. But at this meal, Jesus spoke to them of his own death and promised them a renewed fellowship or communion in the kingdom of God (Mk 14:25). After the crucifixion, the disciples continued the tradition of table fellowship, gathering to break bread and share the cup in memory of Jesus as at Emmaus, and so came to recognize the risen Jesus present among them (Lk 24:13-35).

Priests today who preside at the table of the eucharist in Jesus' name invite others into communion with Christ and with one another. They are called to be ministers of reconciliation and communion. The world we live in today is deeply fragmented. Our families are often divided. Our parishes can easily marginalize those who don't "fit in." Our societies and political communities are divided on the basis of race, sex, social status, the use of power, and the control of wealth. The body of Christ is divided into separate churches.

1. Reconciliation of Churches

At the Second Vatican Council, the Roman Catholic Church committed itself to the search for Christian unity, but too often ecumenism and the concern for reconciliation that is the heart of genuine ecumenism remains the concern of the specialist, rather than of the average priest or pastor.

The search for Christian unity is often impeded by an institutional intransigence on the part of the churches and a profound lassitude on the part of many of their members. But perhaps the greatest obstacle to reconciliation remains the fact that far too few Christians really long for reconciliation. The churches today seem content to live in peace as they follow their separate paths. There is a new level of mutual respect. Occasionally they cooperate on practical matters or come together for common witness. Dialogue is encouraged. But for the vast majority, Christians in different churches remain strangers to each other. Because they have not struggled, lived, and worshiped together, they don't really recognize each other as sharing the same faith.

For the majority of Roman Catholics especially, there is little felt need for reconciliation. Their church is a world-wide communion, their local congregations generally large, their services usually full. In spite of what various commentators have argued about the future of the territorial parish, it remains for most Catholics their primary experience of church. A parish which includes several thousand families, and has four or five masses per Sunday, a host of organizations, and numerous links with the diocese, does not experience any need to reach out to other congregations. Unlike the typically much smaller Protestant congregation, which might number less than a hundred people, the Catholic parish is usually self-sufficient.

Priests as public ministers of the church missioned to act in Christ's name have a special responsibility to be ministers of reconciliation. St. Paul speaks of the apostles as receiving "the ministry of reconciliation" (2 Cor 5:19). If priests who share in the church's apostolic ministry are not themselves concerned for reconciliation and Christian unity, they can hardly be expected to help expand the awareness of their parishioners, so that they might become more conscious of the oneness of the church.

2. *Reconciliation of Peoples*

A related issue is helping others to recognize that the divisions in the church today are not merely confessional. In a very real sense, the divisions resulting from poverty, racism, political oppression, the unequal distribution of wealth and power, and the lack of respect for the full spectrum of human rights are also expressions of the lack of unity of the church. Christians are called to a unity which transcends such divisions as well as the alienation they cause.

Paul rebuked the Corinthians for celebrating the Lord's supper without being mindful of the poor in their midst. Their eucharist was thus not a blessing, but a judgment on themselves (1 Cor 11:17-34), for there is an essential connection between the celebration of the eucharist and love of one's sisters and brothers. If we forget this connection, our religious worship become mere cult. The image of Archbishop Oscar Romero, murdered while he was celebrating mass because of his outspoken advocacy of the rights of the poor, is a powerful contemporary icon of the inseparability of universal love and eucharistic practice.

Today a host of highly charged, emotional questions involving race and ethnic identity, feminism, abortion, gay rights, and so on are increasingly included among justice issues. Not always theological issues, they are rooted in different anthropologies, different personal histories, and different understandings of sexuality. Yet these issues of race, gender, and sexuality cannot be easily separated out from the justice issues they often raise and the religious identities they at least in part constitute. These are also issues calling for reconciliation, ecumenical issues, precisely because Christians are called to a unity which transcends such divisions as well as the alienation and even violence to which such divisions so often lead.

These issues cause alienation both within and across traditions. Dealing with those who feel themselves excluded or oppressed because of them, and with the alienation and anger they are quick to express, is one of the most difficult and taxing tasks a priest today will have to face. These issues can complicate considerably the priest's ministry, but to ignore or contemn those who struggle with them can frustrate the service of reconciliation to which the priest is called.

Ministry as Leadership

In addition to being a ministry of reconciliation, priesthood in the church is a specifically ecclesial ministry of forming and leading the community gathered in Jesus' name. It is a ministry of leadership through word, worship, and service. This is true of priesthood, whether it is exercised in stable communities of faith or is lived out more prophetically, exercising an essentially evangelical ministry or deepening the faith of those already baptized.

Here I would like to single out three critical dimensions

of this task today. First, the priest must be able to give word to the community's experience. Second, the priest must be able to work collaboratively with others. Finally, the priest must also be able to challenge those in the community.

1. Giving Word to Experience

To serve and preside over a community gathered for worship, fellowship, and service, a priest must be in touch with the experience of the members of the community. First of all, he must be a good listener, one who is able really to grasp what is being expressed, not just by the words, but also through the tone and body language which mediate the feelings of the speaker. A priest unable to listen on several levels to his community, or who always approaches others aware only of his own agenda, will not be able to interpret their experience, to give it word and expression. Without this ability to give word to experience, to recognize how God is acting in the community's life and what God is saying to its members, preaching becomes empty rhetoric and liturgy mere ritual.

Giving word to the experience of a community takes place particularly in the homily. As Robert Schwartz has written, in the effective homilist, "Leadership and membership must come together."[8] The most difficult part of preparing a homily is not developing a particular theme, but finding the connection between the good news contained in the text and the experience of the community.[9] What are the concerns of the community members at this moment? What is on their minds? Where are they struggling? A good homily is one that is able to articulate those struggles and concerns. A bad one does not; it addresses the preacher's agenda, like the priest who preaches self-righteously on abortion without ever having personally known a woman who has had one. It is couched in general terms, as though it came straight from the pages of the homily service. Or it simply circles the subject, like a plane unable to find the runway in the fog.

Giving word to the experience of a community means being able to name the negative as well as the positive. Recently, at a funeral mass for someone who had taken his own life, I heard a homily which failed to deal directly with that tragic event which was very much on the minds of all those present. Our preaching and our liturgies have to recognize and make room for the negative.[10] Think of the power of those psalms of lamentation which have given word to the experience of so many over the centuries. It is precisely the tragedy and brokenness of our lives which opens for us the possibilities of God's transforming grace.

A priest isolated from the members of his community cannot hope to give word to its experience. The image of the priest as a "man apart" is not very helpful today. A priest must be able to bring to the role of liturgical presidency the concerns of all those in the community; he must be able to give them expression. A priest whose material needs have always been provided for, who has never had to support himself, will probably not understand those who struggle to support their families. If he has never confronted and been confronted by the experience of those who find themselves on the margins of the community, he will probably not be able to minister to them; he will not be able to give word to their experience.

Giving word to the experience of a community means more than a merely sacramental ministry. It includes articulating a vision of what Christian community means in a secularized world and a deeply divided church. With so many in the church split over sexual, social, and ecclesiological issues, a priest who would articulate such a vision must be able to live with considerable ambiguity, including an ambiguity about the forms the priesthood itself might take in the future.

2. *Working Collaboratively with Others*

Just before the Second Vatican Council, Yves Congar described the prevailing Roman Catholic monarchical ecclesiology in terms of the papal triple-crown tiara. The tiara, which rises from a wide base to a single point at the top, "was an apt expression of the idea of pontifical monarchy and a quasi-pyramidal concept of the Church."[11] The council replaced this monarchical ecclesiology with a collegial one.

A collegial model of church calls for a new understanding of ministry, not just for the pope and the bishops, but for all those who exercise leadership and authority in the church. This is especially true for priests.

The times in which the priest was the most educated member of the American Catholic community are long past. As a sociological group Catholics in the United States are more present in the professions and more highly educated than any other group except for the Jews. Archbishop Rembert Weakland has frequently emphasized that the educational background and new social status of Catholics in the U.S. poses new challenges to their priests and bishops.[12] To be effective leaders priests must be able to work collaboratively with others, with professionally trained lay ministers, with religious women, and with the well-educated lay men and women who sit on parish councils and make up their various committees.

It is rare today to hear the story of a person no longer active in the church because of a bad experience with a priest in confession. Not enough people go to confession today. But who has not heard the stories of those no longer active in the church because of unhappy experiences with priests unable to work collaboratively with others? The number of highly trained lay ministers, many with professional degrees, who are leaving parish ministry today for this reason should be a serious concern.

A priest who is not able to share his authority, to listen to an honest difference of opinion, even to criticism, will be a failure. He must be able to relate to all the different groups within the community and to help them learn to respect each other. He must be able to work collaboratively, to welcome the competence of others, and to seek and build consensus.

Father Philip Murnion, director of the National Center for Pastoral Life, summarizes the range of challenges faced by a pastor today:

> ...the demands on all pastors and, it seems, particularly on inner city pastors are enormous and varied. They range from the need for worship leadership that suits the local culture to the need for administration of often large, old and deteriorating buildings. They involve relationships within the parish, with community and civic groups, and with diocesan offices. They call for biblical faith and vision, secular savvy, empathy with individuals and skills of organizing.[13]

Closely related to working collaboratively with others is the issue of empowerment. Power means the ability to act decisively, to bring about change. Though the concept of power is often perceived negatively today, there is also a positive side to power. As Michael Downey writes:

> Power may tend to corrupt, but it may also enhance life. It may be hoarded or it may be shared. It may be understood as something held in the hands of a few, or it may be viewed as the life and breath of God loose in the world, the Spirit at the heart of all creation.[14]

The reversals proclaimed in Mary's Magnificat (Lk 1:46-55) represent a promise of the empowerment of the lowly in the coming time of fulfillment. There are numerous examples in the gospels of Jesus empowering others through his ministry. He gave the disciples a share in his own ministry, sending them forth to preach: "They expelled many demons, anointed the sick with oil, and worked many cures" (Mk 6:13). Woman were empowered to follow him as disciples (Lk 8:2). A woman he met at a well in Samaria becomes the instrument by which others come to discover him as savior (Jn 4:39). In John's gospel, Jesus says: "I came that they might have life, and have it to the full" (Jn 10:10).

If priests are to build and sustain Christian communities, they must be able to empower others. To do so, they need to recognize the gifts of others so that they might be able to make their own contributions, not just to the life of the ecclesial community, but also in the world where the Christian life is lived out. Priests also need to find ways to include and empower those in their parishes who don't fit into the pattern of the typical family—single adults or parents, gay people, those in interchurch marriages, the divorced and remarried, the widowed.[15]

3. Challenging the Community

Finally, if a priest is to be not just a co-worker but also a leader, he must be able to challenge others, both personally and communally. This prophetic role is rooted in the priest's responsibility for proclaiming the word, but goes far beyond the task of preaching. But, again, a priest cannot challenge others simply on the basis of his office or authority. His words, if not deeply rooted in his own experience and in the integrity of his own life, will not ring true.

A priest who is not a person of prayer will not be able to call others to a prayerful life. If his own life is not nourished by prayer, deepened by contemplation, enriched by spiritual reading, he can hardly recommend these activities to others. Most parishioners recognize instinctively the difference between spirituality and rhetoric, between liturgical prayer and theater.

Similarly, a priest who has had no direct experience with the poor will not be able to challenge others in the area of social justice. The experience of those whose lives have been ruined by violence or even the threat of violence, who are without adequate food, decent housing, educational opportunity, who lack even personal privacy and a stable family life, will remain foreign to him. An "insertion experience" which requires a significant amount of time living and working with the disadvantaged should be an intrinsic part of the training of candidates for the priesthood, if challenging others to a concern for the poor is to be an important part of their ministry. Those who have not walked in the shoes of the poor will not be able to call others to their assistance.

A priest can hardly call others to ministry and service if he has no consciousness of being a servant himself. A priest who avoids the marginalized members of the community, those who are different from him, or those who resent him, cannot be a servant. A priest whose heart is not inclusive, who ministers only to the beautiful people, or to those like himself, who has no time for the lonely, the hurting, or the elderly, is oblivious to those he seeks to serve.

Conclusions

In the gospels Jesus frequently speaks of himself as one who serves, and he calls those who would be his disciples to place themselves last, at the service of others. Edward Schillebeeckx has pointed out that these texts about serving—a number of which are set in the context of a meal—are anchored in what happened at the last supper.

Mark 10:45 speaks of Jesus coming to serve and to give his life in ransom for the many. Luke 22:27, a specific instruction on ministry of local church leaders inserted into Luke's account of the last supper, represents Jesus as saying: "I am among you as the one who serves." In John 13:1-20, Jesus washes the feet of his disciples at the last supper. A variant of this tradition appears in a parousia parable in Luke 13:37b which serves to link the earthly Jesus with the Jesus who will come on the last day. According to Schillebeeckx, the verse "Amen, I say to you, he will gird himself, have them recline at table, and proceed to wait on them," addressed to those servants whom the master finds waiting on his return, presupposes the tradition of the foot-washing.[16]

All ministry is based on the gospel and directed toward the building up of the community. But for those whose ministry includes presiding at the eucharistic table, it is important to note that Jesus' understanding of himself as a servant for the sake of the reign of God came to expression historically at the last supper.[17]

The Christian community continued to gather after his death and resurrection, to break bread and share the cup in memory of his sacrifice. The one who watched over the community also presided at this table of remembrance. The passing of the sacral concept of priesthood, with its clerical and even elitist connotations, should not be regretted. Let us not mourn its passing.

People very much want good priests today, but not priests who seek the ministry because of the prestige or status associated with it. They want priests who can speak to them God's word and who at the same time are approachable, vulnerable like themselves. They sense considerable alienation, in their personal lives as well as in the church, and want priests who can be ministers of reconciliation and communion. They want pastors who are leaders precisely because they are able to work with others, priests who are collaborative rather than dominative, able to help them discover their own gifts and empower them, leaders who can share their experience as well as challenge them.

But the priest is also called to represent Christ to the church, in celebrating the sacraments and particularly in presiding at the eucharist. The eucharist is a powerful manifestation of the presence of the risen Jesus to his own. It speaks to those gathered around the table of remembrance and thanksgiving in many different ways.

As a priest, I've always found the experience of giving out communion at a Sunday mass particularly moving. One sees so much on the faces and in the eyes of those who come forward to receive the body of Christ: pain, struggle, often tears, faithful endurance, a hunger for something more than bread, expectation, hope, sometimes joy. To be present as a minister in these moments of communion is a great privilege.

In the story of the miracle of the loaves—a story which symbolizes both the eucharist and the abundance of the great eschatological banquet in the kingdom—the evangelist tells us that Jesus pitied those in the great crowd that followed them, for they were like sheep without a shepherd (Mk 6:34). As he taught them, he must have been aware of the Father working through him. Allowing Christ to work through him, acting in Christ's name, is also part of the ministry of the priest.

Notes

1. Paul Wilkes, *In Mysterious Ways: The Death and Life of a Parish Priest* (New York: Random House, 1990), pp. 5-6.

2. Walter Kasper, *Jesus the Christ* (New York: Paulist Press, 1976), pp.120-121.

3. Edward Schillebeeckx, *Jesus* (New York: Crossroad, 1981), p. 311.

4. "Reflections on the Morale of Priests," *Origins* 18 (1989) 501.

5. Ibid. p. 500.

6. Ibid. p. 501.

7. Katarina Schuth, *Reasons for the Hope: The Future of Roman Catholic Theologates* (Wilmington, DE: Michael Glazier, 1989), p. 118.

8. Robert M. Schwartz, *Servant Leaders of the People of God* (New York: Paulist Press, 1989), p. 142.

9. See John Baldovin's fine article, "The Nature and Function of the Liturgical Homily," *The Way: Supplement* 67 (Spring 1990) 93-101.

10. See, for example, Michael Downey, "Worship Between the Holocausts," *Theology Today* 43 (1986) 75-87.

11. Yves Congar, *Power and Poverty in the Church* (Baltimore: Helicon Press, 1962), pp. 125-126.

12. Rembert Weakland, "The Church in Worldly Affairs," *America* 156 (18 October 1986) 201-216.

13. Philip J. Murnion, "The Future of the Church in the Inner City," *America* 163 (1990) 482.

14. Michael Downey (ed.), *That They Might Live: Power, Empowerment, and Leadership in the Church* (New York: Crossroad, 1991), p. 1.

15. Ibid. chapter 13, "Looking to the Last and the Least: A Spirituality of Empowerment."

16. Edward Schillebeeckx, *Jesus*, pp. 303-305.

17. Ibid. pp. 303-304.

3. PRIESTHOOD AND AFFECTIVITY

Edward Schillebeeckx, commenting on why the disciples of Jesus did not fast while he was with them (Mk 2:18), maintains that it was impossible to be sad in Jesus' presence. Impressed by Jesus' profound humanity and experiencing a warm fellowship at table in his company, the disciples were completely taken up with him.[1] Certainly Jesus was no gloomy celibate. Jesus was good company. His celibacy did not cut him off from other people, but made him more available to them. The stories in the gospels showing that people felt free to approach him suggest that he was warm and affectionate with them.

Priestly or religious celibacy represents a life of celibacy chosen for the sake of the kingdom of God (Mt 19:12) and modeled on Jesus' life of loving service. Such a life cannot afford to exclude affectivity and intimacy. Since gospel celibacy is a form of discipleship, a capacity for intimacy—for affective relationships—is the sign of a fruitful chastity. As Father Wilkie Au has written: "To gauge how chaste we are, a good practical guideline is the depth and quality of our friendship. To remain at a safe distance from others is not a sign of chastity. On the contrary, it is a kind of un-chastity if it prevents us from involving ourselves deeply and caringly in others' lives."[2]

But living a celibate life is a considerable challenge. Sexuality is a powerful dynamism, deeply rooted in the human person. As a power of loving which literally brings forth life, sexuality expresses itself in a need for intimacy and for generativity. The virtue of chastity seeks to focus the power of sexuality and integrate it into one's state in life. When integrated, sexuality opens one up to the possibility of discovering the mystery of another person and relating to him or her in an intimate and loving way.

Most people learn about intimacy and love through sharing a life together; for many, marriage is the great school of love. Celibates give up the right to a spouse and children of their own. But they also are sexual beings with erotic energies which need to be recognized and chan-neled rather than denied or repressed. Celibates can be warm and tender in their relationships with others; indeed, if they are to love as Jesus did, they must do so. They must foster the ability to be intimate with both men and women without being romantically or erotically involved.[3]

Living a celibate life is not without risk. Celibate living can lead to an avoidance of close relationships. Some celi-bates, fearful of sexuality's explosive power, repress their sexuality, and, with it, the affective dimension of their per-sonalities. They seem to show no affectivity in their relation-ships with others. The affective life of some celibates seems limited to anger. Some build protective walls around them-selves; they become fixated on personal interests. Some seek to dull their longing for children of their own and their need for creative "fathering" and "mothering" by pouring themselves into their work. Addictions of various kinds, alcoholism, workaholism, overeating, compulsive shopping—the "shop till you drop" syndrome—and so forth, can also be signs of an underdeveloped affective life.

Other celibates dissipate their energies in the fruitless search for a relationship which will take the place of the spouse they have given up by their commitment to celibacy. Though they are more honest about their sexual needs than those who deny or repress them, they remain dominated by them. Their affectivity is narrowly channeled, exclusive, not freely given.

Still others in their loneliness find the challenge too much to endure. They enter into clandestine relationships, justifying them in terms of a higher viewpoint or personal need while minimizing the double lives they are forced to lead.

A celibate life is particularly a challenge when it must be lived out in a highly sensate culture which neither understands nor supports it—in other words, a culture like our own which reduces affectivity to desire and intimacy to physical expression.

How can priests help each other to better integrate their affective needs with their celibacy, so that their chastity might be more fruitful for their lives and for their ministries?

There are a number of issues that surface here. First, priests need to be aware of the differences present among them, based on the different seminary or religious formation experiences each one has received. Second, those different formation experiences have a great deal to do with the way they look at questions of affectivity and sexuality. Today these questions often include the issues of sexual identity and orientation. Finally, I would like to suggest some personal questions for all of us, a kind of examination of consciousness in regard to affective relationships, to serve as a check on where we are and how each of us might need to grow.

Religious Subcultures

One of the greatest difficulties priests face in trying to understand and communicate with each other about the issues that touch them most deeply is that they are the products of different religious subcultures. The attitudes imbued in priests through their seminary training or formation, the social patterns learned, the theologies and spiritualities which supported them—all of these shape their experience today, no matter how much they have grown or changed over the years.

In any group of priests today which includes both older and younger men, there are at least three distinct populations which reflect different religious subcultures. First, there are the *Patres Graviores*, those older priests ordained prior to 1965. Second, there are the *Survivors of the '60s*, a middle-aged group whose formation embraced the turbulent years of the Second Vatican Council. They were ordained between 1965 and 1975. Finally, there are the *Younger Fathers*, those ordained in the last fifteen years, from 1975 to the present.

At the beginning, it must be said that the three "ages" of priests presented here are stereotypes, painted with very broad strokes. One cannot predict a priest's attitudes toward affectivity and intimacy simply on the basis of when he was in the seminary. Nevertheless each priest has been deeply influenced by the formation he received. They have all been marked by that experience, even when in later years they have reevaluated or even rejected it. Priests need to ask themselves who they are, and where they have come from. With the recognition that these generalizations are precisely that, not valid in every case, and that there can be considerable overlap between the groups, we will consider each group briefly.

1. The Patres Graviores

It is fairly safe to say that for those who prepared for the priesthood in the years before the Second Vatican Council, affectivity was suspect. Most of them entered seminaries and novitiates at a very young age. Their formation was extremely rigid. Much of the spirituality read in its course reflected a neo-Platonic dualism—often reinforced by a strong dose of Irish Jansenism—which emphasized mind over matter, spirit over flesh, and thought over feeling.[4] The body was the seat of the senses, the appetites, and the imagination, the manifestations of a human nature corrupted by sin which constantly threatened the life of grace. Feelings and emotions came from the flesh, not the spirit. Asceticism meant principally mortification, a self-denial designed to master an unruly and disordered human nature.

Not untypical of this other-worldly spirituality would be the following passage from a work on mental prayer widely read in the two decades prior to Vatican II:

> Mortification should begin with the senses, and when these are taught restraint, not much difficulty will be experienced in controlling the interior. For by the denial of their gratifications to the external faculties, the imagination itself is starved of all that can excite in it pleasant, agreeable, and sensual images. . . . Our sensitive faculties . . . must be submitted to a regular treatment, consisting in a consistent thwarting of their desires. . . . We ought to submit them not only to restraint and privation, but to positive suffering in order to be sure to secure order in their activities.[5]

Notice, not just a disciplined moderation, but a positive deprivation of whatever might stimulate the senses, move the feelings, or enrich the imagination:

> We should mortify our eyes not lending them to the
> gratification of an idle curiosity.... We should mortify
> our sense of hearing by training ourselves to shut our
> ears to what merely pleases or flatters us.... Musicians
> should exercise a check on their desire to hear music,
> should deliberately shut their ears to all that is merely
> sensuous, and should refuse themselves the pleasure
> of hearing again in their imagination the good music
> that appeals to them.... The sense of touch is the most
> dangerous of all the senses and demands an exercise
> of the most rigorous mortification.... We should for-
> bid ourselves any touch that has no other end but to
> yield a sensible gratification—even though that gratifi-
> cation may not be sinful.[6]

The constant fear, usually unspoken, was that to give in to
merely "natural" affections would be to unleash the pas-
sions, and thus to risk falling headlong into serious sin.

With such a negative view of human nature, religious
formation in seminaries and novitiates was designed to be
protective, even custodial. They were usually built in isolated
places, often on hilltops. The presence of women was excluded. Issues of sexual identity were not discussed; indeed, the
term sexual identity would probably not have been understood. Though homosexuality was rarely mentioned, a fear
of it was evident in numerous restrictive rules and regula-
tions. Seminarians and young religious were not allowed to
visit each other in their rooms, or later, in the major seminary or theologate, could do so only if the doors were left
open. They were continually warned against "particular
friendships," exclusive emotional relationships which could
be divisive in community life and possibly pose a threat to
chastity. Recreation was generally in assigned groups.

The all-male environment in which seminarians and
young religious were formed encouraged a rugged individ-

ualism, an anti-intellectual and often competitive "Lone Ranger" spirituality relieved by long walks and lots of athletics. Controversy and open criticism of authority were not tolerated. The endless conversations about sports—usually a safe topic—still heard in many rectories and recreation rooms is an inheritance of this system. At its best, it led to a rough and ready camaraderie which passed for genuine friendship and helped socialize candidates for the priesthood into a clerical culture.

On the negative side, the protective approach did little to foster affective development. Many seminarians, their fantasies influenced by the pervasiveness of their all-male environment, struggled with fears about their own sexual orientation. Later, as priests, they entered their ministry with little experience of women as either equals or friends, and with little capacity for deep friendships with other men. The theology they received stressed a cultic and sacral understanding of the priesthood. Their role as priests was clearly defined and highly valued; it was surrounded with special privileges and signs of respect.

Because these men accepted the spirituality in which they were formed at great personal sacrifice, they often find change very difficult. Some are frustrated in a church so different from the one they knew in their youth. Many are angry. They feel that the rules were changed in the middle of the game.

Many of those who survived have proved to be disciplined and dedicated priests. They have served the church well. But the affective cost has been very high. Because personal issues have been so often suppressed for the sake of what they understood as their vocation, many of them find it difficult today to express their feelings to others, or even to recognize them. They feel awkward in group settings that place a priority on personal sharing. Many will admit today with profound sadness that they have no real friends, even among those with whom they have been living for years.

2. *The Survivors of the '60s*

The second group, those in their middle years, were ordained between 1965 and 1975. Because the majority of them entered seminaries or the religious life before the Second Vatican Council began, they constitute a kind of swing group. Andrew Greeley described them in the early 1960s as the "new breed." Many have experienced the pre-Vatican II church in all its rigor, and they have lived through the changes brought by the council while they were still undergoing their formation and experienced its often unfulfilled hopes.

Though most in this group were still relatively young at entrance, an increasing number were coming now from colleges and universities. They entered a world in which a host of external symbols and customs defined what it meant to be a priest or religious: cassocks or habits, a monastic lifestyle, religious titles, a day marked by the ringing of bells, reading at meals, structured recreation, scrutiny of personal correspondence, assigned prayers and devotions, the Great Silence after 9:00 p.m.[7] But within a few years, that world of external symbols was largely stripped away, often with few external supports offered in its place.

The late 1960s and early 1970s were years of considerable experimentation. As formation programs opened up, seminarians and religious became involved in encounter groups, the peace movement, student protest, and psychotherapy. In reading authors like Martin Buber, Abraham Maslow, and Carl Rogers they became familiar with a new vocabulary of self-actualization through interpersonal encounter.

There was considerable debate over celibacy and the meaning of chastity. One definition frequently heard was that celibate chastity meant precisely celibacy, or, in other words, merely that a priest or religious did not enter into marriage. There was a widespread sense that the rules were changing, a hope not yet fulfilled that the discipline of mandatory celibacy would be relaxed. Many thought it was simply a matter of time. One Irish pub in a major west coast city became famous in the 1970s as a place for "Third Way" gatherings of priests and their women friends for dancing and socializing. For religious especially, summer schools at Catholic universities throughout the country became occasions for meeting the opposite sex and even dating.

For many this time of experimentation, of probing limits, was a liberating experience. Many "fell in love," becoming emotionally involved with women, and discovering that they were called not to celibacy but to the married life, and left their seminaries or communities. Others remained, but with a new sense from the experience that their choice of celibacy was a real one, consciously undertaken. Those who went on to ordination gained a new appreciation of affectivity as it became clear that the new emphasis on interpersonal relations would remain an important part of personal development. Many became more comfortable in relating with women. But on the negative side, many women were hurt or felt used by these relationships.

3. The Younger Fathers

The third group includes those ordained since 1975. They vary greatly in background and experience. A good percentage of them, particularly in the last ten years, have started their training for the priesthood at a much older age. A good number have had considerable sexual experience prior to their entrance into a seminary or religious community. Some have been married. Many religious have done their theology in ecumenical theological unions where they have studied with men and women from other churches and been forced to confront issues such as feminist hermeneutics, inclusive language, diverse understandings of sexuality, liberation theology, and considerable theological pluralism. In some divinity schools today, an ideological agenda focused on minority, feminist and sexual issues has redefined radically the approach to Christian faith and ministry in terms of both pedagogy and practice.[8]

Feminism in particular has changed the way those in this group feel about themselves and their ministry. They have met women who reject much of the church and their own ministry as oppressive patriarchical structures. No longer is their ministry taken for granted and esteemed, and their own motives have been questioned. Ordinations have occasionally become the occasions for protest rather than joyful celebration. Many feel uncomfortable, caught between an institutional church they can no longer entirely defend and a significant group of educated, alienated Catholic women.

The formation programs for those preparing for priesthood today have been generally much more open. Earlier formation programs were based on an incorporational model which judged a candidate's suitability for the priesthood or religious life on the basis of his ability to adapt and conform to the customs and practices of the community.

In recent years, however, a number of cultural currents have helped shape a new approach to formation. Humanistic psychology, reacting to both rationalism and the dominant empiricism in psychology, has focused on the role of affectivity in personal development. Similarly, a new emphasis on intersubjectivity has emerged in both philosophy and theology. A reevaluation of the significance of feelings took place. Rather than being dismissed as irrational, they are now recognized as affective or bodily responses of an organism to its environment.

These currents have led to a new appreciation of the importance of affectivity in prayer, decision-making, and ministry for seminary and religious formation. As a consequence, many recent formation programs have attempted to incorporate a developmental model, stressing the need to develop the candidate's particular gifts and to discover a way to express and live out his unique individuality within the priesthood or religious community. Rather than measuring success by conformity to external norms, they have stressed individual direction, personal choice, and experiential learning, allowing the individual to experiment and to learn from his mistakes. Many have made considerable use of psychotherapy for those with personal problems.

From the beginning these programs have stressed a considerable degree of personal disclosure and interpersonal sharing. Issues of sexuality and sexual identity have been discussed much more openly. For the first time, a significant number of seminarians and religious have been identifying themselves as homosexual in orientation, not only to themselves but to others in their group.[9]

Thus those entering the priesthood today place considerable importance on affectivity. They don't hesitate to raise with pastors and religious superiors the question of their own affective needs. They are much more concerned with issues of psycho-sexual development and personal expression and they are more comfortable in discussing questions of personal identity and sexual orientation. Some feel that the balance has shifted to an overconcern with these issues, while others point out how the lack of psycho-sexual development among priests has been a detriment to their ministry.

Furthermore, the appearance of an admittedly gay group in what had previously been presumed to be a "straight" community has frequently generated both anxiety and homophobia. There are still significant divisions within the priesthood over these issues that need to be addressed. What can we say about affectivity and sexual identity?

Affectivity and Sexual Identity

There have always been homosexuals in the priesthood and religious life, but because sexual identity in the past had generally not been an issue publicly discussed, they did not identify themselves as such. Furthermore, the social climate would not have permitted such disclosure. In recent years, however, a number of factors—among them a new assertiveness on the part of the gay community, a sense of the importance of owning one's sexual identity, and changing attitudes toward homosexuality in general—have led to a new openness on this subject within seminaries and religious communities.

Sexual identity is an important issue, one that consumes a good bit of time and energy. Many priests today are becoming more comfortable with sexual difference. But with this new emphasis on sexual identity have come a number of problems. "Acting out," the trying on and experimenting with one's sexual identity, sometimes in terms of physical, erotic expression, has been a new challenge, for both homosexuals and heterosexuals. As part of this acting out, some gay seminarians have identified themselves publicly with the gay community and taken on elements of the gay subculture in their personal lifestyles, as a way of affirming and valuing what had previously been denied or repressed.

Today it is increasingly clear that priests are members of a mixed community, with both straight and gay members. There is need for considerable sensitivity here, and for respect for the differences in sexual orientation present. Each priest needs to address honestly his own personal phobias, whether homo or hetero. Too often one still hears the putdowns of gay people and dismissive jokes which come under the expression "gay bashing." These should not be tolerated among priests.

At the same time, there is often a cliquishness among self-identified gay priests, along with a ill-concealed contempt for "straights" who are dismissed as insensitive, uncreative, and uninteresting. This kind of reverse stereotyping can be described as heterophobia and is equally offensive.

It is important for each of us to recognize and be comfortable with our sexual identity. But sexual orientation is part of our total identity; it is not or should not be that which defines us. For priests especially to redefine themselves on the basis of sexual orientation is needlessly divisive and usually not helpful to the individual.

A man who defines himself in terms of sexual orientation usually ends up focusing all his energy along those lines.[10] There are many splendid priests who are gay. But a priest who defines himself as a gay priest, rather than as a priest who is also gay, often spends inordinate amounts of time seeking out gay friends, pursuing gay interests, even taking part in gay activities. It is not at all clear that adopting elements of a gay lifestyle or going to gay bars is appropriate behavior for a priest committed to celibacy. The same cautions of course would apply to a heterosexual priest who defined himself and structured his activity primarily in terms of his sexual interests.

For priests committed to a celibate life, their personal

identity should be rooted in their priesthood, not in their sexual orientation. To identify themselves and each other as straight priests or gay priests is to focus on an issue which is not central to their vocation and may indeed distract one from it. Priests are called, like Jesus, to identify with all God's people, not just with those who are like themselves.

Some Personal Questions

Once any of us grants that the affective dimensions of our lives are important, it follows that we should be willing to make some efforts and take some steps to grow in this area of affectivity. In what follows, I would like to pose some questions as a kind of examination of consciousness in respect to our affectivity. They pertain to all people, but in this context, they are raised particularly for priests. They are personal questions, not for public discussion. But they might suggest to each of us areas for further personal reflection.

1. Who is my spiritual confidant?

If we are to remain open to the challenges our experience presents us with and the opportunities for growth to be found there, we need someone with whom we regularly check in, a spiritual director, soul friend, guru, confessor, or best friend with whom we can talk about those things that touch us most deeply. Too often priests, who serve as understanding listeners and free psychiatrists for many hurting people, have no particular person who listens regularly to them. They have many excuses for this. They are too busy, don't have the time, can't find the appropriate director, don't get much out of sacramental penance, and so on.

Some, after years of sealing their deepest concerns within, are simply unable to talk about them with another human being. One priest, in a rare moment of disclosure, consciously identified himself with the Simon and Garfunkel song, "I Am a Rock," commenting on how the song described his own isolation: "I am a rock, I am an island; I touch no one and no one touches me...." How painful such an admission is.

We all need someone who cares enough about us to listen, to give us honest feedback, and able to challenge us. And if there is no one able to do this, we need to ask why. What is our capacity for friendship, for intimacy? Do we put others off, or are we so wrapped up in ourselves, so dominating in conversation, that others flee when they see us coming.

The sacrament of reconciliation could be such an opportunity for a priest. But it is ironic, that while the practice of reconciliation continues to diminish, many lay people who do take advantage of the sacrament have found it to be a unique opportunity for some significant spiritual conversation, some personal sharing on a spiritual level. Indeed, they expect that. At the same time, many priests continue to approach reconciliation merely as an *ex opere operato* event; wanting a quick in and out, they come seeking primarily a juridical absolution.

There are other ways to initiate such an ongoing conversation. Spiritual direction works well for some. Others make it a point to take some time off regularly for a quiet meal with a friend. But what is crucial is to have some regular contact with someone we can talk to and trust.

Without some person to occasionally touch base with, the walls of confinement and isolation remain intact. We manage to make time for those things that really matter to us. Why not for this? We are not rocks or islands.

2. Who are the friends with whom I can be intimate?

Intimacy involves sharing our inner selves with another. In the words of Michael Downey, "Intimacy refers to the desire to be held and to hold, to caress and be caressed, to bathe another in love and be bathed in love. Intimacy describes a union which is inclusive of sharing fears and tears, pain and suffering, thrill and excitement."[11]

The need each person has for intimacy is a profound one. This is equally true of priests. We all need friends with whom we can be intimate, both men and women. But sometimes priests are afraid of intimacy.

One fear may be rooted in the confusion of intimacy with sexuality and physical expression. Unfortunately, our culture is frequently guilty of this confusion. In newspapers and other forms of public communication, the word intimacy often is used as a synonym for sex; to have been intimate with someone is to have had sex with him or her.

There is a sexual dimension to intimacy precisely because an intimate exchange involves two human beings meeting each other on the level of their unique individual identities and personalities, and our sexuality is always an important dimension of who we are. Intimacy involves our feelings and affections. It presumes mutuality and can lead to physical expression. But sexual intimacy is only one kind of intimacy. Intimacy is a measure of the depth of our friendship. It might mean expressing our love and affection in an appropriate way. We are intimate with those we deeply care for, not with strangers, business associates or those we don't like.

Some fear intimacy because it involves personal disclosure. Being intimate with another human being is to be vulnerable; it means opening one's self, and that involves risk. But intimacy also enables us to talk about our feelings—our hopes and our fears, our confusion and frustrations, our relations with others, the longings of our hearts, our relationship with God. It can be a very liberating experience.

It is important for priests to have both men and women as intimate friends. Both support and open them, in different ways. Some priests who are uncomfortable with women or find it difficult to understand their concerns today are precisely those who have never had any real women friends. A priest who relates only to women, or only to men, who excludes from his affections one or the other half of humanity, is emotionally underdeveloped and crippled in his ministry.

3. What community sustains me?

Community is especially important for a priest. Many priests who give up a family of their own find their ministry of shepherding a local community deeply fulfilling. Many religious priests find their own needs for intimacy and generativity realized through a life shared with their brothers in their religious community. They find community life both challenging and fulfilling. But how often is it true that priests whose mission it is to build and lead community are the least familiar with living it?

Of course, the word "community" today is often overused, and can become a cliché. Endless talk about community can create unrealistic ideals or lead to self-centered groups which expend enormous amounts of energy and time seeking to meet each other's emotional needs, without any real challenge to growth. There is no ideal community; rather, good communities are those where their members constantly strive to support and be present to one another.

A community does not happen merely because people who share the same vocation or similar interests happen to live together. It takes considerable effort. Many young people today perceive diocesan priests as living a life with little real experience of community. They see the young priests, closest to themselves in age, living in a rectory with a pastor who is considerably older, both in age and mentality, and perhaps another priest somewhere in between. Too often these priests do not pray together, they take their recreation separately and watch their own TV in their separate rooms. If the old authoritarian pastor is gone, his successor often keeps an uneasy peace in the house by adopting an attitude of disengaged tolerance, out of fear of a bad report to the personnel board.

The situation is not always much better for religious communities today. Too often a combination of theological pluralism with an individualism not uncommon in the religious life has resulted in a community that is chiefly functional; its members are united by a common task to be done and are supported by their pooled resources, not by an experience of unity that grows out of companionship in mission, communal prayer, and shared reflection. The present movement toward small or satellite communities represents an effort to find a more genuinely communal life in a less institutional environment.

Priests today need communities which can support and sustain them in their ministry. A good parish can provide considerable support and satisfaction for a dedicated priest, but parishes are generally very family oriented. Many priests feel the need for a specifically priestly community.

There are some possibilities. Priests from several neighboring parishes could join together for personal sharing and prayer on a regular basis. An alternative might be to meet once a week to share their reflections on the readings for the following Sunday's homily. In areas where the different Christian churches follow a common lectionary, this might be done ecumenically. Some priests gather regularly in support groups which facilitate communication with colleagues and friends on a deeper level. There could be more experimentation with the team-ministry concept, rather than the traditional pastor-assistant model. A base community could develop within a parish, consisting of its ordained and lay ministers, gathering regularly for prayer, perhaps centering on the liturgy of the hours.

4. What are the forbidden areas in my life?

Another question might seek to uncover those areas of our lives that we are afraid to share with those closest to us, the forbidden areas, the ones we fence off with alarms, minefields, and the "DO NOT ENTER" signs. We all have areas we are uncomfortable opening up to those who are closest to us, and sometimes even to ourselves. These are the issues we don't want to discuss even in our diaries or journals. They are explosive because our feelings are involved. They show us where we are most vulnerable. Sometimes these forbidden areas involve issues, the ordination of women, sexuality, authority, addiction. Often they involve painful memories, wounds long suppressed, experiences repressed. Sometimes they involve specific people who have hurt us or threaten us. We often have our own "enemies" list and should be particularly concerned when our personal lists seem to be growing rather than diminishing.

These forbidden areas are our danger zones. However, another way of considering them is to see them as offering rich possibilities for more significant sharing with a trusted friend. These forbidden areas often reveal to us a significant part of our own religious experience; they indicate where we need to grow, where we are being challenged, gently, by the Spirit of God.

Priests who are not able to talk about their own religious experience with another, who cannot share their own personal struggles, their secret fears, are inhibited in their capacity to minister as guides and directors to those who look to them for help in prayer. But how often do priests today open themselves to this kind of ministry, even from one another?

Many priests would like to; they want to be able to share their own loneliness, their struggles with celibacy or their efforts to find the Lord in prayer with someone whose experience is similar. The great appeal of a writer like Henri Nouwen is precisely his ability to be in touch with and share his own inner life with his readers and to discover therein the moments and patterns that reappear in their own personal journeys.[12] The challenge of facing our own forbidden areas and danger zones is that of finding a similar rich field of experience that deepens us as persons and increases our capacity to minister effectively and affectively to others.

5. Do I bring my affectivity into my prayer?

A final question might focus on affectivity and prayer. Often we go to prayer, hoping to experience something on the level of our feelings. We want to know God's love for us, to sense God's closeness or rest quietly in the presence of the one who alone can still the hunger of our hearts. We come with the hope of being moved in our prayer.

But how often do we bring our affectivity into our prayer? Like the man at the pool of Bethesda waiting for the movement of the waters (Jn 5:2-9), we sit waiting for the waters of our heart to be stirred up, without adverting to the currents and movements already there. We try to put our best foot forward, to put on the emperor's clothes, forgetting that God loves us as we are, not as we might like to be.

It is only when we are able to bring into our prayer

our disappointments and struggles, the quiet joy that sometimes illumines our lives from within, the anger that often blocks us, our sexual desires and the longing for tenderness and intimacy which they so often hide, our feelings of emptiness and lassitude, that we are able to stand in utter honesty before the Lord. But when we approach God as we most deeply experience ourselves, we often find that what seems to be the opacity of our spirit becomes a transparency before the Lord.

In the same way, an attentiveness to what we are feeling and experiencing, and, even more, to the mood and emotional quality of the community for whom we are celebrating, can give new life to our liturgical presidency, provided that we are able to bring that awareness to some kind of expression. There should be an easy crossover, a flow back and forth between our private prayer and our liturgical prayer. Good liturgy expresses our experience; it does not simply fashion it. Some priests who have squeezed any affective presence from their presidential style seem to literally "execute" the liturgy. An overemphasis on the language of celebration when a community is experiencing sorrow and confusion renders our liturgical language superficial and empty. We need to make room for the negative in our prayer, both personal and communal, to provide a place for lamentation.

Conclusions

Jesus remains the model for the ministry of priests. Jesus was not just a prophet or teacher. His life enabled him to be uniquely present to all those he encountered, to respond to each person honestly and with affectionate concern. Among his disciples he had some, both men and women, who were particularly close to him. Though he esteemed marriage highly, he himself did not marry, and he saw being single for the sake of the kingdom of God as a way of life enabled by God (cf. Mt 19:11-12).

From the earliest days of the church, men and women have chosen to follow him in single lives as an expression of their discipleship. A celibate life is not an easy life; it has its own particular challenges. First of all, it must be honest. Second, it must open a person up to others. It does not exempt him or her from close relationships with others; nor does it exclude affectivity and intimacy.

Indeed, the whole point of a celibate life is to open one to an non-exclusive kind of love, a tender, warm and compassionate love of others. And there is the real challenge. If celibacy is not lived out as a way of loving, if it does not make a person more tender, warm, and compassionate, then ultimately it is difficult to justify. The challenge is to love as Jesus did.

Notes

1. Edward Schillebeeckx, *Jesus: An Experiment in Christology* (New York: Crossroad, 1981), pp. 201-206.

2. Wilkie Au, *By Way of the Heart* (New York: Paulist Press, 1989), p. 150.

3. According to Bishop Michael Pfeifer, intimacy, even for celibates, "includes relating to people of both sexes.... It is through healthy experiences of intimacy that celibates develop those qualities needed to minister to others, such as gentleness, sensitivity and compassion": "Intimacy, Friendship and the Celibate Lifestyle," *Origins* 20 (May 17, 1990) 16.

4. See James B. Nelson, *Embodiment: An Approach to Sexuality*

and Christian Theology (Minneapolis: Augsburg, 1978), pp. 45-58 for a discussion of dualistic thinking and its influence on the Christian tradition.

5. Edward Leen, *Progress through Mental Prayer* (New York: Sheed and Ward, 1940), pp. 244-245.

6. Ibid. pp. 246-249.

7. See, for example, Paul Hendrickson, *Seminary: A Search* (New York: Summit Books, 1983).

8. See the provocative article on contemporary seminaries and divinity schools, Protestant, Catholic and Jewish, by Paul Wilkes, "The Hands That Would Shape Our Souls," *The Atlantic Monthly* 226 (December 1990) 59-88.

9. For a survey of recent institutional attempts to address this issue see Robert Nugent, "Homosexuality and Seminary Candidates," in *Homosexuality in the Priesthood and the Religious Life*, ed. Jeannine Gramick (New York: Crossroad, 1989), pp. 200-218.

10. See, for example, *Gay Priests*, ed. James G. Wolf (San Francisco: Harper & Row, 1989).

11. Michael Downey, *Clothed in Christ: The Sacraments and Christian Living* (New York: Crossroad, 1987), p. 148.

12. See, for example, Henri J. M. Nouwen, *The Genesee Diary* (Garden City, NY: Doubleday, 1976).

4. PRIESTHOOD IN APOSTOLIC RELIGIOUS COMMUNITIES

In a recent article, John O'Malley has argued that the traditional categories used to describe religious priesthood are inadequate and lead to a confusion harmful to religious life. Though the confusion is deeply rooted, O'Malley sees it still present in the Second Vatican Council's decree on priests, *Presbyterorum Ordinis,* a document which assumes that all priests are ministering by and large to the faithful, exercising that ministry in stable communities of faith, in hierarchical union with the bishops.[1] The problem that O'Malley has singled out here is that the model chosen as paradigmatic of priesthood is that of the diocesan clergy.

Priesthood in the church admits of a variety of types and forms, diocesan, monastic, and apostolic religious. The priesthood of a secular or diocesan priest, a parish priest or pastor, is most often a ministry of word, sacrament, and pastoral leadership within a local church community, whether on the parish or the diocesan level. Monastic priesthood, exercised most often in a monastery under the jurisdiction of an abbot, is focused on the *opus Dei* or liturgy. It provides a model of a priesthood which is less clerical, more communitarian, and characterized by a monastic restraint in liturgical celebration.[2] The priesthood of a religious priest belonging to an apostolic religious order or community is different from both of these types of priesthood.

In this chapter we will consider priesthood in apostolic religious communities. We will focus on three orders which historically have been exemplars of an apostolic religious priesthood, the Franciscans and Dominicans, both founded early in the thirteenth century, and the Jesuits, founded toward the middle of the sixteenth century. They are not the only religious communities which exercised a priesthood different in kind from that of the local or diocesan clergy. Other mendicant communities such as the Carmelites and the Augustinians were founded in the thirteenth century. Similarly, the sixteenth and seventeenth centuries saw a number of new apostolic religious communities, clerks regular like the Theatines, Barnabites, and Piarists as well as Capuchins and Vincentians. But the Franciscans, Dominicans, and Jesuits are the best known and were perhaps most influential in developing a new expression of religious priesthood.

Priesthood: Cultic and Prophetic

The Catholic understanding of priesthood combines into one office two religious roles which the history of religions has seen as conceptually distinct, that of priest or cult official and that of prophet. The priestly role is one of presiding over the ritual expression of a community's religious experience. In this way, the priest leads the community in addressing itself to God. The prophet on the other hand is the one through whom God's word is addressed to the community.

This conceptual distinction of roles has been useful for purposes of religious study and description, even if it may overlook a deeper coincidence in the biblical tradition on an existential level. But in the Christian tradition, from the time of the early Christian prophets and teachers, the cultic has been rooted in the prophetic. Those who came to be called priests preside at the eucharist because they have instructed the community through the word and exercised a presiding role within it. In terms of Catholic theology, they have been authorized to preach in the name of the church. Thus the church's pastoral office cannot be reduced to a purely cultic function.

Yet as Michael J. Buckley has suggested, the actual way priesthood is lived out in the concrete life of the church has sometimes tended more toward a cultic expression and at other times tended more toward a prophetic expression.

In an article written for scholastics preparing for ordination in the Society of Jesus, Buckley sketched the differences between a cultic and a prophetic priesthood. A cultic priesthood is characterized by an emphasis on sacramental ministry and the liturgical prayer of the choral office. It describes the responsibility of the ordained monk whose life is devoted to the *opus Dei*, the cathedral canon who has responsibility for the liturgical and sacramental ministry of a major church, as well as the parish pastor or priest who presides over the liturgical and sacramental life of a local congregation.

A Prophetic Priesthood

A prophetic priesthood is a priesthood given to the ministry of the word in its fullest sense. It is primarily kerygmatic rather than liturgical, though it does not exclude the liturgical. Unlike priests whose ministry is focused on the leadership of stable local communities, those exercising a prophetic priesthood must be available for mission. In Buckley's words:

> A prophetic priesthood, one which was concerned to speak out the word of God in any way that it could be heard, assimilated, and incarnated within the social life of human beings, a priesthood which spoke with the religious experience of human beings and—as did the prophets of the Old Testament—coupled this care for authentic belief with a concern for those in social misery: the ministry of the word, the ministries of interiority, the ministry to social misery.[3]

For Buckley the Society of Jesus is characterized by such a prophetic priesthood. The Jesuits, as a clerical order, represented a new form of the ancient *presbyterium*; they were a group of priests with a primarily prophetic mission. But they were not the first such community in the history of the church. Three centuries earlier, the Franciscans and the Dominicans, influenced by a twelfth century evangelical movement known as the *vita apostolica*, developed a new form of priesthood which was primarily prophetic or kerygmatic in orientation.

1. Dominicans and Franciscans

Both Francis of Assisi and Dominic de Guzman were influenced by the great evangelical awakening which swept through Europe in the twelfth century. Both established communities which sought to embody the values of the *vita apostolica*,[4] living in poverty and simplicity like the apostles, free to go where there was need, preaching the gospel in the towns and cities.

The movement begun by Francis was originally lay in orientation. But from the beginning, preaching was basic to his understanding of his vocation. He began preaching in Assisi in 1209, the day after hearing the priest celebrating mass at the Portiuncula on the feast of St. Matthew read from Matthew 10:7-9:

> As you go, make this proclamation: "The kingdom of heaven is at hand." Cure the sick, raise the dead, cleanse lepers, drive out demons. Without cost you have received; without cost you are to give. Do not take gold or silver or copper for your belts; no sack for the journey, or a second tunic, or sandals, or walking stick. The laborer deserves his keep.

Soon others joined him, wandering the countryside with him and preaching in the towns and villages. In the early days, his companions were sometimes mistaken for members of other evangelical fraternities—particularly the Waldensians—whose orthodoxy was suspect. At the same time, as uneducated, itinerant preachers, they were in danger of falling into doctrinal heterodoxy themselves.

Part of Francis' achievement was his success in keeping his movement within the church. His "Second Rule" or *Regula Bullata* was approved by Honorious III in 1223, giving his community the status of a religious order. The community began to place an increasing emphasis on religious formation as well as on formal education. But as the movement became more structured, his "lesser brothers" underwent a clericalization which in large measure was necessitated by the requirements of their preaching mission. It is believed that Francis himself was later ordained a deacon.

The Dominican first order was clerical from the beginning. Dominic was a priest, a cathedral canon, but a rather untypical one. What kind of priesthood did he envision for his order?

Most formative for Dominic was his itinerant ministry with his bishop, Diego of Osma, in their struggle against the Albigensians in southern France. The Dominican order grew out of the group of missionaries who joined Dominic. They lived an itinerant life, owning only what they could carry with them, and supporting themselves by begging, all for the sake of the proclamation of the gospel.

Simon Tugwell relays a story, originally told by an early Dominican preacher. When Dominic requested that Pope Innocent III recognize his new community as an Order of Preachers (*Ordo Praedicatorum*), the pope wondered to himself why this man wanted to found an order consisting entirely of bishops. The pope was confused because it was still assumed that bishops were the only official preachers.[5] Whether the story is true or not, it is particularly instructive. Preaching in the thirteenth century was not seen as the ordinary role of priests; they assisted the bishop by carrying out a sacramental ministry in local churches, but the bishop was the official preacher. Priests were primarily cultic ministers.

But Dominic, in identifying his largely clerical community as an order of preachers, was opting for what we have called a prophetic priesthood. The ministry of his followers was not to be modeled on that of the regular clergy who had authority over local communities as well as financial claims upon them. The priesthood he intended was something new, a specifically active or apostolic form of clerical religious life focused on a preaching ministry. The preaching mission given his order by Honorius III in 1217 was unprecedented, as was the general mission of hearing confessions entrusted to the order in 1221. The preaching mission was derived from the exempt character of the order's priests as evangelical assistants to the bishops and the pope, rather than from the responsibility of bishops and pastors to preach or to see that sermons were preached in their churches.

Dominic had adopted for the members of his community the apostolic life, based on Luke 10. What was needed was clear preaching of the gospel. Dominican structures and lifestyle, including their emphasis on poverty, developed from the pragmatic task to be done. Everything was subordinated to this. The nuns and lay brothers, present from the beginning, apparently shared in this task by providing a material and spiritual base for the preachers. Catherine of Siena, a third order Dominican, is reported to have told her confessor repeatedly that her greatest consolation was talking about God with others.[6]

Dominican spirituality followed from the mission. Because of the community's apostolic orientation, regular observance was always secondary. Dominic sent his followers far and wide, to preach and later to study. The constitutions were understood as human law, not binding under pain of sin. Superiors could give dispensations from traditional monastic observances, including choir, which interfered with preaching or study. Though the order had to struggle in its early days to defend its preaching ministry, separated from the responsibilities of pastoring local communities, it won the right to be acknowledged as an order of preachers, just as Dominic intended it to be.

Thus, the Franciscan and Dominican movements produced a new kind of religious order in the church, exercising a new kind of priesthood. As O'Malley has pointed out, the mendicant priests differed from the local or diocesan clergy in a number of significant respects. First, influenced by the *vita apostolica* and committed to poverty, very early the friars combined spirituality and ministry into an apostolic lifestyle. Second, because of their emphasis on preaching, they began a systematic program for the education of their new members. Third, their ministry, geared to respond to needs that transcended local boundaries and jurisdictions, required them to move about "like the apostles." In other words, their ministry was itinerant, characterized by mobility. This meant a break with existing church structures of government.

Finally, this unique ministry was recognized from the beginning by papal exemptions from episcopal supervision. The monastic orders also enjoyed an independence from episcopal control, but unlike Cluny, Cîteaux, and other monastic communities, the mendicants received exemption, not just for their own governance, but precisely for the sake of their wide ranging ministry.[7] As O'Malley puts it, this development "created in effect a church order (or several church orders) within the great church order, and it did this for the reality to which church order primarily looks—ministry."[8] What had emerged was a new kind of priesthood, freed from the confines of episcopal jurisdiction or monastic enclosure, precisely for the sake of the word, a prophetic or kerygmatic priesthood.

2. The Jesuits

In the sixteenth century, the Jesuits represented another group of priests with a similar pastoral mission. On September 27, 1540, Pope Paul III canonically established the Society of Jesus with his decree *Regimini militantis Ecclesiae*. The decree recognized the first ten Jesuits as a single apostolic "body" or "presbyterium," grouped not around a bishop as head of a diocese, but around the pope for the service of the universal church. The Formula of the Institute describes the Jesuit vocation as a willingness to go wherever they were sent, under special obedience to the pope:

> In addition to that ordinary bond of the three vows, we are to be obliged by a special vow to carry out whatever the present and future Roman pontiffs may order which pertains to the progress of souls and the propagation of the faith; and to go without subterfuge or excuse, as far as in us lies, to whatsoever provinces they may choose to send us—whether ... among the Turks or any other infidels, even those who live in the region called the Indies, or among any heretics whatever, or schismatics, or any of the faithful.[9]

From the beginning Jesuits were travelers. Francis Xavier departed for what was then referred to as "the Indies" in 1540, the year the Society was officially approved as a new religious order. By 1556, the year Ignatius died, there were Jesuits working in India, Japan, Brazil, and Africa. Jerome Nadal, Ignatius' secretary, described the Society of Jesus as most itself when on the move, so that "the whole world becomes its house."[10]

There were significant differences between the mendicants and the Jesuits. Dominican priestly life was to be rooted in liturgy and contemplation. But as the traditional form of such a communal life in the thirteenth century, even for canons, was essentially monastic, there was a monastic dimension to Dominican life from the beginning, though mitigated by Dominic's emphasis on the priority of preaching. Similarly the Franciscans took on some monastic practices as they developed.

Ignatius' community was unique for its time because it was established without a distinctive habit, prescribed fasts and penances, or the obligation of the choral office. The omission of choir was to cause some problems for Ignatius and the early Society; those appointed in Rome to examine the Institute as Ignatius presented it could not conceive of a religious order whose members did not gather regularly for the office. But Ignatius wanted his priests to be mobile.

Thus Jesuit priesthood was not primarily cultic. In addressing the Society's mission, *Regimini militantis Ecclesiae* mentions preaching the gospel, both to believers and to unbelievers (what we would call today evangelization) and the sacrament of reconciliation. It did not mention the eucharist, even if the mission of a priestly order includes the celebration of the eucharist.

Though his own spirituality was profoundly eucharistic, Ignatius did not insist that each Jesuit celebrate daily, nor did he always do so himself. But Jesuits were to attend mass daily. In the Jesuit tradition (at least until concelebration became common) a Jesuit on the day of his last vows generally did not say mass, but attended and received communion from the one receiving his vows.

Their priesthood was prophetic, a priesthood focused on preaching and evangelization. As O'Malley points out, what dominates the early Jesuit sources is the ministry of the word. Jesuits were preachers, not just at mass, but in the church outside of the liturgy as well as in the streets and hospitals. They wrote books to aid preachers with examples from classical literature and the fathers of the church. They gave sacred lectures and taught catechism to children. They went on "missions," both foreign and domestic, reclaiming a sense of "journey" or "pilgrimage" for the word "mission" which had been previously confined almost exclusively to trinitarian theology. They gave retreats and were involved in spiritual direction. They established a network of schools to carry out their religious mission. And they were active in what we now call "social" ministries, working with the poor and the sick and establishing houses for reformed prostitutes.[11]

The Jesuits were not the only religious priests to exercise a prophetic priesthood. The sixteenth century saw the establishment of a considerable number of clerical communities, among them the Barnabites, the Theatines, the Capuchins, and the Vincentians. All were dedicated to an apostolic life, based on the various ministries of the word.

3. Loss of a Prophetic Focus

However a number of factors in the centuries that followed the period of origins for these various religious communities served to change the prophetic understanding of their priesthood into a more traditional cultic one. Some communities underwent a process of monastification. The process of institutionalization that the Dominican community went through in the several generations that followed Dominic's gave it an increasingly monastic character.[12] The Dominican liturgical rite, developed under the administration of Humbert, the fifth master general of the order, reflected monastic usages. Its maintenance as a rite distinct from the Roman ritual until after the Second Vatican Council contributed to a more cultic understanding of priesthood within that community.

Another important factor leading to a loss of the prophetic focus and to a more cultic understanding of priesthood was the theology of priesthood which emerged from the Council of Trent. Behind it stands the figure of St. Thomas Aquinas. Like other medieval theologians, Thomas defined priesthood in terms of sacramental power, a *sacra potestas* which stressed the priest's cultic role rather than his relation to a particular ecclesial community, as we have already seen. Thomas did not ignore the ministry of preaching; he treats it along with confession and study in his articles on religious life in the *Summa Theologiae*.[13] He assumed that preaching was the responsibility of religious orders like his own, though subject to the authority of the pope and respectful of the bishop's authority in his diocese.

But his failure to mention preaching in the context of the priesthood was to have unfortunate consequences in the subsequent history of Roman Catholic theology. His theology of the priesthood was confirmed by the Council of Trent and was passed down through the subsequent manualist tradition to our own time. Those preparing for the Catholic priesthood prior to the Second Vatican Council learned their theology from these manuals. Unlike the reformation traditions which focused on the pastoral office as a preaching office (*Predigtamt*) or ministry (*Dienst*), Roman Catholic theology continued to focus on the priesthood in terms of the sacred power the priest possessed which enabled him to consecrate or "confect" the eucharist. Such an approach reduced priesthood theologically to a cultic function.

4. The Triumph of the Solitary Mass

Nowhere is the cultic concept of priesthood more clearly seen than in the tradition of the private mass, and ultimately, in more recent times, the practice of celebrating mass alone, without either congregation or the presence of another member of the faithful.

According to Joseph Jungmann, a private mass is a mass celebrated for its own sake, with just a server, or sometimes with no one in attendance.[14] Schillebeeckx traces the origin of the private mass to the practice of the veneration of relics in the sixth century, a practice requiring the presence of a priest who would read the mass at the altar containing the reliquary.[15] Other authors see the private mass originating in the monasteries, where the growing number of priest-monks from the eighth century on led to the practice of daily private mass. By the ninth century private masses and votive masses for particular intentions had become well established.

According to Jungmann, in the eighth and ninth centuries mass was sometimes celebrated without the presence of even a server. But from the ninth century on new legislation appears which is aimed at preventing this *missa solitaria* or solitary mass. He cites a number of texts and canons which require the presence of others, *ministri* or *cooperatores*, not so much for the sake of assisting "but rather that someone is present as a co-celebrant, so that the social, plural character which is so distinctly revealed in the liturgy we actually have . . . might be safeguarded."[16]

Since at least the time of Pope Alexander III in the twelfth century, the prohibition of celebrating mass without the presence of some member of the faithful has been a matter of church law.[17] And so it remained up until shortly after the Second Vatican Council. The Missal of Pius V repeats the requirement that a cleric or someone else be present to serve.[18] The 1918 Code of Canon Law specifically prohibited celebrating without a server: "*Sacerdos Missam ne celebret sine ministro qui eidem inserviat et respondeat.*"[19] According to a number of popular commentaries, celebrating without a server was a mortal sin.[20] Pre-Vatican II Roman directives repeat the requirement of a server or the presence of at least one member of the faithful.[21]

In 1949, the Sacred Congregation for the Discipline of the Sacraments responded to requests for the faculty to celebrate mass without a server in its instruction *Quam Plurimum.* According to the Congregation, authoritative authors recognized only the following exceptions: when necessary to give viaticum to a sick person, to satisfy the precept of hearing mass for the people, in time of pestilence when a priest would otherwise have to abstain from celebrating for a considerable time, and when the server leaves the altar during the mass. The Congregation pointed out that outside these cases, permission for mass without a server was given only by apostolic indult, especially in mission lands. And it noted that Pius XII had ordered the addition to the indults of the phrase, "provided that some member of the faithful assist at the sacrifice."[22] Thus Pius XII wanted it made clear that even if there was no server, some member of the faithful had to be present.

It was only in 1966, after the Second Vatican Council, that exceptions to the rule against solitary celebrations began to appear. Following the 31st General Congregation of the Society of Jesus, Jesuit priests outside mission regions received permission to celebrate mass *in casu necessitatis* without the presence of a server.[23] The faculty was given primarily for private chapels in Jesuit houses to which the faithful were not ordinarily admitted. It thus allowed solitary celebrations of the eucharist.

Similarly, the General Instruction of the 1969 Roman Missal and the 1983 Code of Canon Law mitigated somewhat the prohibition against the solitary mass. No. 211 of the Instruction says, "Mass should not be celebrated without a minister except in case of serious necessity." Canon 906 states: "A priest may not celebrate without the participation of at least some member of the faithful, except for a just and reasonable cause." But the qualifying phrases cannot be interpreted as meaning simply the preference or convenience of the priest.

Canon 906 should be interpreted against Vatican II and the teaching of Paul VI.[24] *Sacrosanctum Concilium*, the Constitution on the Sacred Liturgy, states that rites which are to be celebrated in common, especially the mass, should be preferred to "a celebration which is individual and quasi-private."[25] Interpreting canon 906 in the light of the council and other liturgical documents suggests that the mere preference of the priest is not a sufficient reason for a solitary celebration. Paul VI taught that private celebrations are permissible "for a just cause ... even if only a server assists and makes the responses."[26] The implication is that the presence of at least a server is required. Thus the ancient recognition that the eucharist is the church's prayer and not a private priestly ritual still finds expression in church law.

The "private mass" has a history in the church that reaches back to at least the sixth century. Whatever might be said about the theological appropriateness of private celebrations, the practice was received by the western church as a legitimate expression of eucharistic piety. In this sense the practice could be considered traditional. However the cultic concept of the priesthood to which the private mass contributed is problematic theologically because it focuses on the relationship between the priest and the eucharist rather than on the relationship between the priest and the community.

But if the private mass is a practice of long standing, solitary celebrations of the eucharist, without the presence of at least a server or some other member of the faithful, have been almost universally prohibited by church law. Indults have sometimes been given for mass without a server in mission territories, but Pius XII required at least some member of the faithful to be present.

In recent years, for many religious priests the solitary mass has become their most frequent experience of eucharist. They find their own priesthood most clearly expressed in those quiet moments when they celebrate alone. This is a personal matter, something they apparently find meaningful, and should be respected.

But from the standpoint of the church's tradition, the solitary mass represents a eucharistic practice which has almost no justification. Theologically, the private mass and ultimately the triumph of the solitary mass have played an enormous role in changing the primary prophetic priesthood of many active religious communities into one much more cultically conceived and experienced.

A Prophetic Priesthood Today?

Today there is an increasing emphasis on the ordained minister as the liturgical leader of a local community. The phenomenal growth of the *comunidades eclesiales de base* or base Christian communities in Latin America and elsewhere has raised the question of ordaining the lay leaders who pastor them.[27] There is a prophetic dimension to the ministry of these grassroots community leaders who proclaim the word to their communities and help them find consensus on its implications. On the other hand, the fact that their ministry is localized within a particular community and entails a pastoral care and liturgical/sacramental leadership not unlike that of most parish priests means that their ministry, precisely as community leaders, has a strongly cultic and administrative character.

There is still a need in the church for a priesthood more prophetic than cultic in its orientation. Many clerical religious institutes whose priesthood in its inspiration has been prophetically conceived are questioning today the forms which their ministry should take in the future. It might be worthwhile to attempt to sketch the contours of such a priesthood. A prophetic priesthood would be an evangelical or kerygmatic priesthood. Structured by the requirements of preaching the word wherever it might be heard, it might involve the following:

1. Mobility

Preaching the gospel wherever Christ needs to be proclaimed requires mobility. The early Franciscans and Dominicans were wandering preachers. Dominic intended his community to be a highly mobile group; they were not to be tied down to traditional ministries. Thus he "left his Order, at least at first, with a definite instinct against the official cure of souls."[28] According to Humbert, preaching was to take precedence over other spiritual exercises, including the mass, confessions, the celebration of the sacraments and the divine office.[29] Dominic succeeded in realizing for the first time "a way in which the itinerant, non-territorial, priestly apostolate could be institutionalized."[30] Much the same could be said for Francis, though for his community the struggle to institutionalize his charism was a long and divisive one.

The early Jesuits were understood as reformed priests, free to go wherever they were missioned, with the availability symbolized by the fourth vow of special obedience to the pope. For this reason, certain missions were originally excluded. In the words of the *Constitutions*:

> Because the members of the Society ought to be ready at any hour to go to some or other part of the world where they may be sent by the sovereign pontiff or their own superiors, they ought not to take a curacy of souls, and still less ought they to take charge of religious women or any other women whatever to be their confessors regularly or to direct them. [31]

Today many apostolic orders have lost much of their mobility because of their commitments to established works. Their founders did not intend them to be tied to places, institutions, dioceses, or countries. Even less should they be wedded to a particular social class or culture. A prophetic priesthood needs to be free to go where there is need.

2. Evangelization

A priesthood structured by a commitment to the word of God is essentially evangelical. Unfortunately the Catholic Church today has largely given up the work of evangelization to Protestant evangelicals. In the United States the Catholic Church has hardly begun to address the challenge of evangelization in an affluent and secular culture. What Mary Catherine Hilkert has said about the directions that preaching the gospel should take for Dominicans today applies equally to other communities with a prophetic charism: "The growing strength of fundamentalism, the political power being exerted by the new right in religion, and the vast areas of this country which are classified as 'unchurched' all call for a response on the part of an order founded specifically for the proclamation of the gospel."[32]

Hilkert's parallel between the United States today and France at the time of Dominic is very much to the point. The Catholic Church both in the U.S. and in Latin America is losing millions of Hispanics to evangelical and pentecostal churches. When challenged about "proselytizing" or "sheep stealing," evangelical representatives have responded, with considerable truth, that these Hispanic Catholics "have been sacramentalized but not evangelized."

But Catholic representatives could equally well respond that these evangelical and pentecostal churches too often offer an individualistic and privatized Christianity which is not the full gospel. Part of the genius of both Francis and Dominic was their ability to find a place within the church for the evangelical movement of their day. A prophetic priesthood could serve Catholicism in a similar way today. The church needs effective evangelism, one able to combine a faith both personal and ecclesial with a concern for justice. The need for this among Hispanic Catholics is particularly acute.

3. Social Justice

The church in the late twentieth century has become increasingly aware of the social dimensions of the gospel and its proclamation. The 1971 Synod of Bishops stated explicitly: "Activity on behalf of justice is a constitutive dimension of the preaching of the gospel."[33] In the renewal of religious life which followed the Second Vatican Council, a considerable number of religious communities have sought to make a commitment to justice and solidarity with the poor an intrinsic part of their mission. That commitment should also characterize a community whose priesthood is prophetic in orientation. Furthermore, working for justice is one particularly significant way that non-ordained members of a community can share with the ordained in expressing in their own ministries the community's charism for preaching or in its prophetic priesthood.

4. The Intellectual Life

In spite of the fact that neither Dominic nor Ignatius foresaw the commitment to the intellectual life which would come to characterize their communities, both communities became involved in higher education and scholarship even within their founders' lifetimes. The Franciscans also became involved in university education early in their history. In each case, this involvement was a direct result of their efforts to provide a quality education for their own junior members. The mendicants stressed education precisely because of their preaching mission. Their members were soon studying and teaching at the great universities of Europe. Ignatius set up houses or "colleges" at the better universities of his day for his scholastics. Soon the lectures these colleges provided drew other students who sought admission.

Both the Dominican and Jesuit constitutions reflect the high value their founders placed on solid intellectual formation. Dominic provided dispensations from community observances for the sake of study as well as preaching. Part IV of the Constitutions of the Society of Jesus are devoted entirely to Jesuit colleges and universities. Ignatius saw the development of any human talent or gift as useful for the sake of the order's mission. Because of this, his order became synonymous with a lengthy intellectual formation. By the time of his death in 1556, the number of Jesuit colleges had already grown to forty-six. By the early seventeenth century, the Jesuits were staffing more than four hundred educational institutions.

A religious community whose priesthood is prophetic in orientation can neglect the intellectual life only at the expense of its ministry of the word. Teaching belongs to the mission of the priest. If the gospel is to penetrate and illumine a complex, technological culture such as our own or be able to challenge the pervasive secularism of contemporary western societies, it will take minds which are not just highly trained, but insightful and cultivated. This demands an emphasis on higher education and a commitment to the intellectual life. The alternative is a non-dialogical fundamentalism. A prophetic priesthood cannot afford to neglect the intellectual life, even for the sake of its commitment to social justice. Particularly in this area, anti-intellectualism can easily lead to an ideological blindness which is destructive of genuine reconciliation.

Conclusions

The church's priesthood can admit of variations and subdivisions in its organization. It also has various expressions. Given the shortage of priests in the church today and the growing need for local community leaders, able to celebrate the eucharist, the church of the future will probably see more forms of priesthood, rather than fewer. The religious orders, both monastic and apostolic, with their own forms of priesthood, have and will continue to enrich the church with their witness and their ministries. It would be a tragic mistake to attempt to force a redefinition of their priesthood in order to address the current shortage of ordained pastors.

The gospel must be proclaimed and interpreted, not just in the context of parishes and local communities, but to the church itself, to the complex cultures in which it lives, to the millions who are unchurched today, and to those on society's margins. There is and will continue to be a need for a prophetic priesthood, evangelical in orientation, free to move where needed, skilled at bringing the word of God to bear in all its many dimensions—preaching, teaching, carrying out the guiding ministries of spiritual direction and the prophetic ministries of social justice. This kerygmatic or prophetic priesthood is how the priesthood of many active religious congregations should be understood.

Notes

1. John W. O'Malley, "Priesthood, Ministry, and Religious Life: Some Historical and Historiographical Considerations," *Theological Studies* 49 (1988) 223-224.

2. See, for example, Kevin W. Irwin, "On Monastic Priesthood," *American Benedictine Review* 41 (1990) 225-262.

3. Michael J. Buckley, "Jesuit Priesthood: Its Meaning and Commitments," *Studies in the Spirituality of Jesuits* 8 (1976) 150.

4. Cf. Thomas P. Rausch, *Radical Christian Communities* (Collegeville: Liturgical Press, 1990), pp. 62-83.

5. Simon Tugwell, "Introduction," in his *Early Dominicans* (New York: Paulist Press, 1982), p. 14.

6. Simon Tugwell, *The Way of the Preacher* (London: Darton, Longman & Todd), p. 23.

7. O'Malley, '"Priesthood, Ministry, and Religious Life," pp. 233-237.

8. Ibid. p. 236.

9. Ignatius, *Constitutions*, 4; George Ganss, *The Constitutions of the Society of Jesus* (St. Louis: Institute of Jesuit Sources, 1970), p. 68.

10. Cited by John O'Malley, "To Travel to Any Part of the World: Jeronimo Nadel and the Jesuit Vocation," *Studies in the Spirituality of Jesuits*, 16 (1984) 7.

11. See O'Malley, "Priesthood, Ministry, and Religious Life," pp. 239-241.

12. See Tugwell, *The Way of the Preacher*, pp. 82-83.

13. *Summa Theologiae*, II-II, 188, 4,5.

14. Joseph A. Jungmann, *The Mass of the Roman Rite: Its Origins and Development*, Vol. I (New York: Benziger Brothers, 1950), p. 215.

15. Edward Schillebeeckx, *The Church with a Human Face* (New York: Crossroad, 1985), pp. 159-160.

16. Jungmann, *The Mass of the Roman Rite*, p. 227.

17. *Corpus Juris Canonici* c. 6, X, I, 17.

18. *Missale Romanum, De defectibus in celebratione Missarum occurrentibus*, X, no. 1.

19. *Codex Juris Canonici*, can. 813.

20. Joanne B. Ferreres, *Compendium Theologiae Moralis*, Vol. II (Barcelona: Eugenius Subirana, 1919), p. 296; Antonio M. Arregui, *Summarium Theologiae Moralis* (Westminster: Newman, 1944), p. 385.

21. See, for example, *Mediator Dei, Acta Apostolica Sedis* 39 (1947) 557.

22. *Quam Plurimum, Acta Apostolica Sedis* 41 (1949) 507-508.

23. *Acta Romana,* 14 (1966) 753.

24. Cf. *The Code of Canon Law: A Text and Commentary,* ed. James A Coriden, Thomas J. Green, Donald E. Heintschel (New York: Paulist Press, 1985), pp. 647-648.

25. *Sacrosanctum Concilium,* no. 27 in Walter Abbott, *The Documents of Vatican II* (New York: America Press, 1966), 148.

26. *Mysterium fidei, Acta Apostolica Sedis* 57 (1965) 761-762.

27. See Leonardo Boff, *Ecclesiogenesis: The Base Communities Reinvent the Church* (Maryknoll: Orbis Books, 1986), p. 63.

28. Tugwell, *The Way of the Preacher,* p. 17.

29. See Tugwell, *Ways of Imperfection* (Springfield: Templegate, 1985), p. 140.

30. Tugwell, *The Way of the Preacher,* pp. 82-83.

31. Ignatius, *Constitutions,* 588; Ganss, pp. 262-263.

32. Mary Catherine Hilkert, "The Dominican Charism: A Living Tradition of Grace," *Spirituality Today* 38 (1986) 155.

33. "Justice in the World," Statement of the 1971 Synod of Bishops (Washington: USCC, 1972) 34.

5. THE FULLNESS OF THE PRIESTHOOD: THE EPISCOPAL OFFICE AND TOMORROW'S CHURCH

We saw earlier that the Second Vatican Council, in ascribing the fullness of the priesthood to the bishop (LG 26, 28), represented a return to the understanding of both priesthood and orders that developed in the patristic church. It is also true, as Kenan Osborne points out in his book on the priesthood, that this emphasis on episcopacy as the fullness of the sacrament of orders "has a dual implication: one inward to the Roman Catholic community itself, and one outward to the Christian community generally."[1] In this final chapter we will consider the episcopal office as the fullness of the priesthood, briefly, in the theology of Vatican II, and, at greater length, in the contemporary ecumenical dialogue as it relates to the larger Christian community.

Episcopacy in the Theology of Vatican II

The council's teaching on the collegial nature of the episcopal office marked a major breakthrough. Bishops are not to be regarded as vicars of the pope; they govern particular churches with power they possess in their own right (LG 27). In union with the bishop of Rome, they are joined together to constitute a college or body which exercises supreme authority over the universal church, particularly at an ecumenical council (LG 22). Although the episcopal office must be exercised in communion with the head and members of the college, admission of newly elected members is by sacramental ordination (LG 21).

Episcopacy and the Universal Church

One implication of this collegial understanding of the episcopal office is a new understanding of the universal church. The church catholic is not a single, monolithic institution divided into dioceses and archdioceses. The church is a communion of churches.

Some years ago the late patriarch of the ecumenical movement, Willem A. Visser 't Hooft wrote an important article on teachers and the magisterium.[2] In it he argued for the recognition of theologians as a distinct fourth office in the church, next to bishops, priests and deacons (or pastors, elders, and deacons). His solution is probably too Reformed or Presbyterian to be acceptable to the Roman Catholic Church. The bishops as pastors are authentic teachers, identifying and safeguarding the apostolic faith (LG 25).

But the issue he singles out remains a key one. The Roman Catholic Church has not yet really acknowledged that the teaching authority of the hierarchy is not able to function independently of the entire ecclesial community which constitutes the church. The church is not fundamentally an institution, exercising teaching authority from the top down. It is in its essential nature a community in which all members are mutually interdependent. The traditional doctrine of the *sensus fidelium* and the ecclesial reality of reception in the life of the church both imply a mutuality or interdependence between official teachers and the body of the faithful.

Recently, J. Robert Dionne has illustrated this mutuality and interdependence in a convincing manner.[3] In the case of the ordinary papal magisterium Dionne shows how a number of consistent teachings of Pius IX and his successors were ultimately modified or reversed by the Second Vatican Council because of the "modalities" of their reception by theologians. Among these teachings he includes Pius IX's apparent inability to find any truth or goodness in non-Christian religions, his condemnation of the proposition that church and state should be separated, and his denial of religious freedom as an objective right, as well as Pius XII's exclusive identification of the Roman Catholic Church with the mystical body of Christ.[4]

Second, Dionne shows that when the extraordinary papal magisterium was exercised in the definitions of the immaculate conception (1854) and the assumption (1950), in both cases the proclamations were made only after a process of consulting the church through a polling of the bishops.[5]

Dionne's study is important because it illustrates that even in exercising teaching authority the church functions as a communion. As he says at the end of his study, the distinction between the *ecclesia docens* (teaching church) and *ecclesia discens* (learning church) may not be as clear-cut as was previously supposed.[6] Leonardo Boff has made this point even more strongly. He argues that *docens* and *discens* are two functions of one community; they cannot be understood as two parts or divisions within the church.[7]

Episcopacy and the Priesthood

A second implication of a collegial understanding of the episcopal office pertains to the priesthood of presbyters, which also has a collegial dimension. The council deliberately did not use the expression "college of priests." But as Osborne points out, in the documents of the council the stress on priestly collegiality is clear.[8]

The council speaks of priests as "cooperators" with the episcopal order and "co-workers" with the bishop (LG 28). They are bound together in a priestly order by the their ordination. Together with their bishop, priests constitute a "presbyterium" (PO 8; CD 28). While the college of bishops carries a responsibility for the universal church, the presbyterium of bishop and priests carries on a shared ministry in the local church.

Thus there is a relationship of interdependence between a bishop and his priests. As in the early church, bishops should regard their priests as their "counselors" in the ministry and each diocese should have a presbyteral council (PO 7). At the same time, if the bishop is to look upon his priests as his sons and friends (LG 28), then in a real sense among his most important roles is that of pastor to his priests. David Power cites the words Bishop William of Durand (d. 1296) addressed to his priests as being typical of the role of the bishop for many centuries: "I am your pastor, you are the pastors of the people."[9]

Episcopacy in the Ecumenical Dialogues

The question of the episcopal office has come increasingly into focus in the ecumenical dialogues. Begun since the council's conclusion, the dialogues have as their ultimate goal the restoration of communion between and among the various churches. The dialogues have discussed questions such as the nature of the ordained ministry, recognition of ministries, authority, apostolic succession, and the episcopal office. In the process, a common theology of the episcopal office is emerging, along with suggestions for its shared exercise which could lead to a reconciliation of ministries.

At the same time, the dialogues also show a growing ecumenical consensus in regard to those issues related to ordained ministry which have been disputed historically between the different churches. To focus on the episcopal office in ecumenical dialogue is to bring into focus an ecumenical understanding of ordained ministry, and thus of the priesthood. How then is the episcopal office understood in these ecumenical dialogues?

The Dialogues

To answer this question, we will examine five key ecumenical documents which deal with the episcopal office. The first, the ARCIC *Final Report*, marked with its appearance in 1982 the end of the first phase of the work of the Anglican-Roman Catholic International Commission.[10] The *Final Report* includes the ARCIC I agreed statements on eucharistic doctrine (1971), ministry and ordination (1973), and authority in the church (1976, 1981), as well as a number of subsequent "elucidations."

Second, the WCC Lima Text, officially titled *Baptism, Eucharist and Ministry*, or BEM for short, brought to fruition fifty years of reflection on the part of the Faith and Order Commission.[11] Unanimously accepted by Faith and Order at the Commission's meeting in Lima, Peru, January 1982, BEM represents a "convergence" of thinking on the part of the Commission's Orthodox, Protestant, and Roman Catholic members. It must still be received by the WCC's member churches.

Third, we will consider the document of the Roman Catholic-Lutheran Joint Commission, *Facing Unity: Models, Forms and Phases of Catholic-Lutheran Church Fellowship*.[12] Since the Roman Catholic-Lutheran Working Group was reconstituted in 1973 as the Roman Catholic-Lutheran Joint Commission, it has been concerned with finding ways to translate agreement into practical steps toward unity. Over the years, the Commission has produced "The Eucharist" (1978), "All Under One Christ" (1980), "Ways to Community" (1980), "The Ministry in the Church" (1981),[13] "Reciprocal Admission to the Eucharist" (completed in 1982 but not yet published because it lacks unanimous endorsement by the Catholic participants), "Martin Luther—Witness to Jesus Christ" (1983),[14] and *Facing Unity* (1985). The question of the episcopal office as a specific issue has always been present in the Lutheran-Catholic dialogues, but it has begun to surface with increasing urgency.

Fourth, *The COCU Consensus*. The Consultation on Church Union, established after an exploratory meeting in 1962, published an ambitious document in 1970, *A Plan of Union for the Church of Christ Uniting*.[15] The document, calling for full organic unity, did not draw a favorable response from the COCU churches. In the years that followed, COCU shifted from the model of organic union to a covenantal principle, proposed by Gerald Moede, as an interim step toward whatever form of visible unity might someday emerge.[16] A revised approach, *The COCU Consensus: In Quest of a Church of Christ Uniting*, was finally approved by a COCU Plenary session at Baltimore in 1984.[17] The document acknowledges its debt to BEM at certain points in its section on ministry.

Finally, the Anglican-Lutheran *Niagara Report*.[18] Anglicans and Lutherans have been in conversation with each other on different levels for almost twenty years. Wide agreement had been found to exist in regard to doctrine, worship, mission, and the understanding and functioning of the ministry. But the one obstacle which continued to emerge was that of the practice of *episcope*, especially in relation to the historic episcopate. The *Niagara Report* is the result of an international consultation which took place in Niagara Falls, Ontario in September 1987 to address this issue.

Since the documents we are considering are not focused specifically on the episcopal office and have different concerns, we will approach them using five reference points.

1. *Structure of Ministry.* How do the documents understand the ordering of the church's ordained ministry and what position do they take in regard to the episcopal office?

2. *Episcope.* The 1973 ARCIC statement *Ministry and Ordination* summarized the various New Testament images describing the ministry of leadership and church unity with the concept of *episcope*, literally, oversight, which it identified as an "essential element in the responsibility of the ordained ministry."[19] Here we are concerned with the authority and function of the office of bishop.

3. *Historic Episcopate.* This issue, understood as "an episcopate which traces its origins back through history to at least the end of the second century" (*Niagara Report*, no. 3), is particularly important for Anglicans and Roman Catholics. It also raises the questions of apostolic succession in the ordained ministry and the recognition of ministries.

4. *Teaching Authority.* What, if any, teaching authority is granted to the episcopal office? This is especially important for Roman Catholicism, which understands the bishops of the church as exercising a teaching office.[20]

5. *Structural Reform.* A number of dialogues which indicate a positive appreciation of the episcopal office also make clear that the way in which episcopacy is exercised needs to be reformed. We need to consider the reforms proposed and to ask: Can they be received by the churches that need to make them?

Since ecumenical documents are increasingly developed with reference to other ecumenical statements, we will consider them in chronological order.

Five Reference Points

1. *Structure of Ministry*

In the ARCIC *Final Report*, the statement *Ministry and Ordination* simply notes that the threefold ministry of bishop, presbyter, and deacon emerged in its fullness after the apostolic age and then became universal in the church (no. 6). BEM notes that though the New Testament does not prescribe a single pattern of ministry, the threefold pattern emerged in the context of the local eucharistic community and became established throughout the church in the second and third century (M nos. 19-20). BEM and the *COCU Consensus* speak of the threefold ministry as both an expression of unity and as a means for achieving it (M nos. 22, 25; COCU no. 42).

The function of bishops according to BEM is to "preach the Word, preside at the sacraments, and administer discipline in such a way as to be representative pastoral ministers of oversight, continuity, and unity in the Church" (M no. 29).

The 1981 Roman Catholic–Lutheran document, "The Ministry in the Church," was developed with special reference to the episcopacy, seeing lack of agreement here as an obstacle to Lutheran-Catholic communion. It mentioned the desire of the Lutheran reformers in the sixteenth century to retain the episcopal polity of the church and spoke of the installation of ministers by non-episcopal ministers as an "emergency situation" (no. 42).

The Anglican-Lutheran *Niagara Report* advances this

issue considerably. In its opening paragraphs the *Niagara Report* points to differences over the presence or absence of bishops in the historic episcopate as the chief and perhaps only remaining obstacle to full communion between Anglicans and Lutherans (no. 3). The differences include the significance attached to the presence of bishops in the historic episcopate in a church (no. 4). Indeed, much of the report can be read as a polemic against the notion of "linear succession to the apostles as the sole criterion of faithfulness to the apostolic commission" (no. 20).

But from a review of the development of ministerial structures in the church some important clarifications emerge. First, the report identifies in the office of the bishop "the tension between locality and universality."

> In virtue of his election he represented the Christian people of his own town for the universal Church; and in virtue of the assent of the larger Church, symbolized by the mode of his ordination, he represented for his own flock the universal people of God, the whole body of local churches knit together in the communion of Christ (no. 49).

The report sees the bishop as fulfilling a twofold symbolic function, linking the local church with the *koinonia* or communion of the universal church, and linking it with its foundations in the prophetic and apostolic scriptures. Thus the bishop symbolizes the connection between the local and the universal, as well as between the present and the past (no. 52). This connection between the universal and the local is essential to the life and mission of the church (no. 53)

Second, the report argues, using the Roman Catholic-Lutheran Joint Commission's statement, "The Ministry in the Church," that apostolic succession in the episcopal office "does not consist primarily in an unbroken chain of those ordaining to those ordained, but in a succession in the presiding mission of a church which stands in the continuity of apostolic faith" (no. 53).

Third, though both Anglicans and Lutherans claim the succession of a presiding ministry, which in the Lutheran case is present in the pastors, the report acknowledges that "the succession in the presiding ministry of their respective churches no longer incontestably links those churches to the *koinonia* of the wider Church" (no. 58). This is a significant admission.

2. *Episcope*

Authority in the Church I speaks of "the *episcope* of the ordained ministry" as a specific gift of pastoral authority which "belongs primarily to the bishop." The bishop is described as having general oversight of the community (no. 5) which under the bishop constitutes a local church (no. 6). But *episcope* is not understood as a monarchical function. The earlier document on *Ministry and Ordination* describes *episcope* in the context of the threefold ministry: "Presbyters are joined with the bishop in his oversight of the church and in the ministry of the word and the sacraments. . . . Deacons . . . assist in oversight" (no. 9). Thus there is clearly a *collegial* dimension to the exercise of *episcope*. *Episcope* is ordered toward maintaining the apostolicity of the church: "This responsibility involves fidelity to the apostolic faith, its embodiment in the life of the Church today, and its transmission to the Church of tomorrow" (no. 9).

Conciliarity and primacy are complementary elements of *episcope* which need to be kept in a proper balance (*Authority in the Church I*, no. 22). The conciliar principle is traced back as far as the "Council" of Jerusalem (Acts 15), the earliest example of different churches coming together to resolve matters of mutual concern.

The 1981 Roman Catholic-Lutheran Joint Commission document, "The Ministry in the Church," made a breakthrough with implications for the concept of *episcope* when it pointed out that the Catholic emphasis on apostolic succession in the episcopal office finds its meaning in a concern to maintain the communion of the catholic and apostolic church, rather than being understood primarily as an unbroken chain of ordinations (no. 62), behind which lies the old argument about the transmission of sacramental power. Though it did not use the word *episcope* in this context of a concern for the continuity of the apostolic faith, the *Niagara Report* six years later would make this connection explicitly.

BEM roots *episcope* in the New Testament. The apostles exercised *episcope* over the whole church; later Timothy and Titus exercised it over a given area, and still later bishops began to exercise *episcope* over several local communities (M no. 21). Relating it to a concern for unity, BEM says every church needs a ministry of *episcope* in some form (M no. 23).

The *COCU Consensus* brings out clearly the role of bishops as overseers of the church's life and as symbols of its unity; it defines them as "representative pastoral ministers of oversight, unity, and continuity in the Church" (no. 45). They have "general pastoral oversight" for all in their dioceses or jurisdictions (no. 51c). As servants of unity they have an obligation "to call the churches to the goal of visible unity in one faith and one eucharistic fellowship" (no. 51g). At this point, the *COCU Consensus* is clearer than BEM on the bishops' responsibility in regard to Christian unity.

In reviewing the development of ministerial structures in the church, the *Niagara Report* came to see in the office of the bishop "the tension between locality and universality" (no. 49). From this a clarification of the notion of *episcope* emerged. Basic to the function of *episcope* is maintaining the continuity of the apostolic faith (no. 54), and by implication—though this might be more clearly indicated—the communion between the local and the universal church. The report then draws the obvious conclusion at the end of the first chapter: "In the light of the symbolic position of the bishop as reflecting both the universal and the local *koinonia,* the continued isolation, one from another, of those who exercise this office of *episcope* in our two Churches is no longer tolerable and must be overcome" (no. 59). The remainder of the report draws some conclusions and makes some recommendations on the basis of this deeper understanding of *episcope.*

3. The Historic Episcopate

From the beginning, ARCIC has linked the historic episcopate with a concern for church unity. Besides presiding over local churches, bishops in the historic episcopate symbolize ritually (we could say sacramentally) and maintain the unity and apostolicity of the church. In joining in the ordination of a new bishop, they signify that the new bishop and the new bishop's church are within the communion of churches and in continuity with the original apostolic church. This twofold symbolization and maintenance of the communion of the churches, in space and time, comprises for ARCIC the essential features of apostolic succession (*Ministry and Ordination,* no. 16).

BEM offers a nuanced argument for the recovery of the historic episcopate. It argues that the succession of bishops became one of the ways in which the apostolic tradition was expressed, and that it was understood as "serving, symbolizing and guarding the continuity of the apostolic faith and communion" (M no. 36). Though BEM's language at this point reflects that of ARCIC, some commentators have criticized it for failing to develop more adequately the responsibility of the episcopal office for maintaining the communion of the universal church.[21]

BEM sees the episcopal succession "as a sign, though not a guarantee, of the continuity and unity of the Church" (M no. 38), and suggests that those churches which lack it "may need to recover the sign of the episcopal succession" (M no. 53b). What BEM cannot accept is the idea that a ministry should be considered invalid until it enters the line of the episcopal succession (M no. 38).

The historic episcopate has always been a point of tension between Roman Catholics and Lutherans. As early as the 1980 "Ways to Community" document, the Roman Catholic-Lutheran Joint Commission began to address it by raising the question of a shared exercise of the episcopal office. Specifically it spoke of a "possible mutual readiness to enter the fellowship of the historic episcopacy or of the Petrine office" (no. 88) as well of "institutionalized cooperation between the leaders of both churches" as a step toward a common episcopacy (no. 89).

"The Ministry in the Church" document of 1981 made several points in regard to the mutual recognition of ministry. First, as we saw above, it pointed out that the Catholic emphasis on apostolic succession in the episcopal office finds its meaning in a concern to maintain the communion of the catholic and apostolic church (no. 62). In other words, it is an expression of *episcope.*

Second, in interpreting the Second Vatican Council on ministry in the reformation churches, the document argues that the *defectus* in the sacrament of orders in the reformation churches referred to by the Decree on Ecumenism (no. 22) could be understood as meaning "a lack of the fullness of the church's ministry," rather than as a complete absence of it (no. 77).

Finally, Lutheranism approaches the question of the

mutual recognition of ministries differently. According to the Augsburg Confession VII, it is sufficient (*satis est*) for the unity of the church that the gospel be preached in its purity and the sacraments be rightly administered (nos. 79-80). This is interpreted not as a final statement, but as a basic one which, when so understood, can free Lutherans to ask what form of church structure could most effectively support the life and mission of the church and also "face up to the call for communion with the historic episcopal office" (no. 80).

If communion with the historic episcopacy is seen as a possibility in the 1981 document on ministry, the 1985 *Facing Unity* document acknowledges it as a need, but only as part of the process of the mutual recognition of ministry. The document stresses that the lack of the sacrament of orders claimed by the Catholic Church cannot be overcome by theological agreements or ecclesiastical decisions: "What is needed, rather, is acceptance of the fellowship in ecclesial ministry, and this, ultimately, means acceptance of the fellowship in the episcopal ministry which stands in apostolic succession" (no. 98). In other words, the stated goal is a joint exercise of *episcope.*

The document recommends a phased process which could lead to a common ordained ministry and to fellowship in the episcopal office. First, there should be some preliminary forms of the joint exercise of *episcope,* realized through joint working groups, mutual participation in church synods, working relationships between church leaders, and common consultations and decisions (nos. 120-122).

Second, with a fundamental consensus on faith and sacraments, there should be a mutual act of recognition of ministry. The Catholic side would affirm the presence of the ministry instituted by Christ in the Lutheran churches "while at the same time pointing to a lack of fullness of the ordained ministry as a *defectus* which, for the sake of church fellowship, has jointly to be overcome" (no. 124).

Third, the two traditions will begin to exercise a single *episcope* in collegial form; this will include joint ordinations (no. 127).

Finally, the joint exercise of episcopal authority particularly in ordaining would lead over time to the development of a common ordained ministry (no. 132) with an episcopal authority which could be expressed in several different forms: a single *episcope* in collegial form, a single bishop for both communities, or the merger of communities into a single church under a single bishop (nos. 142-145). This last case might be appropriate in a non-Christian environment where both churches find themselves in a minority status.

The *COCU Consensus* also commits itself to a recovery of the historic episcopate. While noting that some churches have a succession of ministers who combine the functions of both bishops and presbyters, it states that "The participating churches intend that in the Church Uniting bishops shall stand in continuity with the historic ministry of bishops as that ministry has been maintained through the ages, and will ordain its bishops in such a way that recognition of this ministry is invited from all parts of the universal Church" (no. 48).

The authors of the *Niagara Report* conclude that they cannot "commend uncritically either the reappropriation of historic episcopate or the perpetuation of existing forms of the exercise of *episcope*" (no. 81). They propose some specific steps to move beyond the present impasse, to be considered below under "structural change."

4. Teaching Authority

This issue is perhaps the most difficult one. It cannot be adequately addressed without also considering the suggestions for structural reform, to be considered below.

ARCIC states that the "bishops are collectively responsible for defending and interpreting the apostolic faith" (*Authority in the Church I*, no. 20). This teaching function, when exercised in regard to the "central truths of salvation" at an ecumenical council, binds the whole church (no. 20).

BEM, as Catholic commentators have noted, is virtually silent on the subject of the teaching authority of bishops.[22]

The 1981 Catholic-Lutheran statement "The Ministry in the Church" singled out the need to "rethink the problem of the teaching office and the teaching authority" (no. 56). The suggestion that Lutherans and Catholics might enter into a joint exercise of episcopal authority is a step toward meeting that need.

The *COCU Consensus* recognizes a teaching responsibility of bishops: they are "a sign of, and are particularly responsible for, the continuity of the whole Church's Tradition . . . as well as of its pastoral oversight . . . as they teach the apostolic faith" (no. 46). As teachers of the apostolic faith, they "have a responsibility, corporately and individually, to guard, transmit, teach, and proclaim the apostolic faith . . . [and] to interpret that faith evangelically and prophetically in the contemporary world" (no. 51b).

The *Niagara Report* recognizes the corporate teaching role of bishops in conference and encourages consultation with others skilled in communications (no. 106).

5. Structural Reform

The ARCIC *Final Report* recognizes the possibility of lay participation in conciliar assemblies (*Authority in the Church I*, no. 9; *Authority in the Church II*, no. 33).

BEM tempers its openness to the episcopal office with a strong emphasis on the need for a more "personal, collegial, and communal" exercise of ordained ministry. It should be personal, to effectively point to the presence of

Christ among his people. The term collegial emphasizes that ordained ministers belong to a college sharing a common task. They must work together. The communal dimension underlines the need for the "community's effective participation in the discovery of God's will and the guidance of the Spirit" (M no. 26).

If there is a need for a ministry of unity at both local and regional levels, the text also stresses that all members should be able to participate in the life and decision-making of the community either actively or through "representative synodal gatherings" (M no. 27). According to Geoffrey Wainwright, the experience of synodal gatherings may be one of the main contributions of the more "Protestant" churches.[23]

The Roman Catholic-Lutheran *Facing Unity* document implies several times that the episcopal office must be reformed. It stresses that the exercise of authority by church leaders does not exclude the responsibility of the laity or the principle of synodal or conciliar government (no. 112). Furthermore, it emphasizes that the doctrinal decisions of church authorities need to be received by local churches, congregations, and believers (no. 60).

The *COCU Consensus* acknowledges that it seeks to incorporate "Catholic" and "Protestant" concerns as well as the experience of its different polities in its approach to ministry (no. 22). This is perhaps most evident in its emphasis on shared government: "Lay persons, bishops, presbyters, and deacons share in the governance of the Church locally, regionally, and nationally" (no. 26f). In reviewing BEM's description of ministry—here in the context of all ministries—as personal, collegial, and communal, the document expands the principle of collegiality beyond its traditional meaning; for COCU, collegiality refers to the relationships between those in different ministries as well as between those in the same ministry. Collegiality means "shared responsibility" and a "partnership in governance" which involves clergy and laity together (no. 22b).

There is a strong congregationalist element in the COCU statement, with its stress on lay participation in church governance at all levels. Churches with strong episcopal traditions may ask if the bishop's authority is more than symbolic; others might be uncomfortable with the document's failure to differentiate the ways in which bishops and "other ministers ordained and unordained" participate in ordinations (no. 51e; cf. no. 37). Do lay people participate in the ordinations of bishops and presbyters by laying on hands? This would be contrary to the apostolic tradition.

No doubt there are other points that will have to be refined. There is still a provisional quality to the COCU statement. On the other hand, like the RC-L *Facing Unity* statement, it suggests a way to bring previously divided churches together with a joint ministry of oversight which shares in the historic episcopate.

The *Niagara Report* also makes some concrete recommendations toward structural change. It calls for Anglican and Lutheran recognition of each other as sister churches (no. 83) and for formal recognition of each other's ministries (no. 86). The Lutheran churches are asked to make four changes in their current practice. Those who exercise an ordained ministry of *episcope* should receive the title bishop. They should be elected until death, retirement, or resignation terminates their tenure. They should receive the laying on of hands from at least three bishops, with Anglican participation after full communion is established; thus it is an ordained episcopal office. Finally, only bishops should preside at ordinations of clergy (nos. 89-92).

The Anglican churches are asked to make three

changes. They should make the necessary canonical revisions to recognize the authenticity of the Lutheran ministries. They should establish structures for reviewing and evaluating the bishop's ministry. And they should invite Lutheran bishops to participate in the laying on of hands at the consecration of Anglican bishops, as a symbol of real interaction in *episcope* (nos. 94-96).

Thus Anglicans will recognize the ordained ministry in the Lutheran churches, the Lutherans will take on an ordained episcopal office where it is lacking, in communion with other—in this case Anglican—bishops, and both churches will enter into full communion. The approach here is similar to that of *Facing Unity*, a phased process which moves from a recognition of authentic ministry to a shared exercise of the episcopal office and to fellowship in the historic episcopate.

An Emerging Consensus

1. There is an increasing recognition in the dialogues we have been considering that the exercise of *episcope* involves more than a mission of overseeing and presiding over local churches. *Episcope* involves also the responsibility of symbolizing and maintaining the communion of the local church with the apostolic church and with the communion of churches which ARCIC identified in 1973 as the role of the bishop (*Ministry and Ordination*, no. 16). The 1987 *Niagara Report* acknowledged that while the Anglican and Lutheran churches had preserved presiding ministries, those ministries no longer linked their churches to the *koinonia* of the wider church (no. 58).

2. A clear consensus is emerging that tomorrow's church will have bishops who will preside over local church-

es and link those churches with the communion of churches. The ARCIC *Final Report* presupposes the episcopal office. BEM, *Facing Unity*, COCU, and the *Niagara Report* make a case for its recovery in those churches from which it is lacking.

3. The Roman Catholic-Lutheran Joint Commission and the Anglican-Lutheran Continuation Committee have suggested a phased process toward reconciliation and the restoration of communion through a shared exercise of the episcopal office.

4. Apostolic succession in the episcopal office is understood as a sign, not a guarantee, of the unity and continuity of the church (BEM, M no. 38). As the 1981 RC-L document "The Ministry in the Church" noted, the *defectus* in regard to ordained ministry in the Protestant churches noted by the Second Vatican Council could be understood as meaning "a lack of the fullness of the church's ministry," rather than as a complete lack of it (no. 77).

5. With a fundamental consensus on faith and the sacraments, this process toward reconciliation could begin with a mutual recognition of ministries. The Catholic Church could do this without necessarily granting that a particular ministry realizes the fullness of the church's ordained ministry (*Facing Unity*, no. 124). This should be done without any suggestion of reordination or mutual validation.

6. On the other hand, if the ministry of bishops in a particular church is to be recognized by all parts of the universal church, it must ordain its bishops in such a way as to invite this recognition (cf. *COCU Consensus*, no. 48). The *Niagara Report* (no. 91), in proposing that Anglican bishops

should participate in the ordination of new Lutheran bishops, suggests a way for inviting this recognition. Such a joint ordination would also lead to fellowship in the historic episcopate.

7. The *Final Report* (*Ministry and Ordination*, no. 16) and the *Niagara Report* (no. 91) have made considerable progress in arguing that bishops should receive their office through the laying on of hands, not merely through appointment. The laying on of hands by several bishops, representing the *koinonia* of the church, suggests the sacramental nature of the episcopal office.[24]

8. The teaching office of the bishops is acknowledged in principle, but not always in the way it is exercised. ARCIC, COCU, and the *Niagara Report* recognize that bishops exercise a teaching office, particularly when they are gathered in conferences or conciliar assemblies. BEM and *Facing Unity* need to address this issue more clearly. *Facing Unity* begins to do this by suggesting that Lutheran and Catholic bishops enter into a joint exercise of episcopal authority.

9. While a willingness to accept the office of bishop is increasingly evident, it is clear that such an office will not be acceptable without a reform of the way that episcopal authority is exercised. All the consultations reviewed here address in different ways the question of the reform of structures and recognize the possibility of the participation of laity and clergy in ecclesial teaching and decision-making structures. ARCIC recognizes that clergy and laity can participate in regional or worldwide councils. BEM and the RC-L statement *Facing Unity* refer to a synodal principle which provides for lay involvement. COCU speaks of shared responsibility at all levels of church life.

Conclusions

Without wishing in any way to jeopardize the importance of the primacy or its place in the church, the fathers at the Second Vatican Council chose an ecclesiology of collegiality and communion over the prevailing monarchical, institutional self-understanding of the Catholic Church. A collegial understanding of the episcopal office has helped with the recovery of an understanding of the church as a communion of churches. Even in the exercise of the church's teaching authority, the church functions as a communion. There is an interdependence between the bishops and the faithful as well as an interdependence of the bishops and the pope within the episcopal college.

There is also an interdependence between the bishops and the priests who together make up the presbyterium of the local church. Priests assist the bishop as counselors and co-workers, while in a real sense the bishop can be understood as the pastor of his priests.

A surprising degree of theological consensus on the nature and role of the episcopal office has emerged in the ecumenical consultations we have reviewed. It does not seem presumptuous to suggest that tomorrow's church will include a shared episcopal office. The steps necessary for the reconciliation of ordained ministries and the restoration of communion have already been indicated. But the agreements reached present specific challenges to each of the traditions.

Anglican, Roman Catholic, and Orthodox churches are called to recognize the authenticity of ordained ministry in non-episcopal churches. Protestant churches which have begun to reflect more deeply on the authority of those whose role it is to oversee and preside over the preaching and sacramental life of the church will have to take steps to put in place a presiding ministry or episcopal office which can link their churches with the wider communion of the church. They will also have to ordain their bishops in a way that will invite their recognition by the universal church. In this way, those churches entering into fuller communion will be able to share the exercise of the historic episcopal office.

However the steps toward renewal indicated by the dialogues are not always easy ones to take. It is not sufficient to develop ecumenical agreements between theologians and church representatives. Bishops and church leaders must also be willing to take the steps toward unity that have been indicated.

In the United States, the Episcopal and Evangelical Lutheran (ELCA) churches were on the verge of doing so, and thus of entering into full communion. But in March 1991, the ELCA Conference of Bishops voted 45 to 12 to recommend to the denomination's church council that "no action be taken by the ELCA until there is agreement that the doctrine and practice of this church are not compromised."[25] Some Protestant church leaders, objecting to the emphasis on the episcopal office in the dialogues, object to what they call a "fundamentalism of polity."[26]

It remains to be seen if the churches will be willing to take the necessary steps toward unity. Yet all the churches are challenged to renew their structures in the light of the tradition and to ensure, in the words of BEM, that their authority is exercised in a more personal, collegial, and communal manner.

This is particularly a challenge for the Roman Catholic Church and the Orthodox churches which are hierarchical in their government. There are significant examples of the participation of theologians and others in ecumenical councils in church history which are precedents for a more inclusive exercise of teaching authority for the church of tomorrow.[27] The Roman Catholic and Orthodox churches will have to consider ways of including representatives of the lower clergy and laity in their structures of teaching and decision-making.

There are still some problems to be resolved on the level of practice. But on a theological level, there is a broad consensus emerging on the nature of the episcopal office. With this growing theological consensus and with a number of concrete proposals toward unity in place, the churches might begin to identify the non-theological factors which remain as obstacles preventing positive steps toward reconciliation. This may present an even greater challenge.

Notes

1. Kenan B. Osborne, Priesthood: *A History of the Ordained Ministry in the Roman Catholic Church* (New York: Paulist Press, 1988), p. 325.

2. Willem A. Visser 't Hooft, "Teachers and the Teaching Authority: The Magistri and the Magisterium," *The Ecumenical Review* 38 (1986) 152-202.

3. J. Robert Dionne, *The Papacy and the Church: A Study of Praxis and Reception in Ecumenical Perspective* (New York: Philosophical Library, 1987).

4. Ibid. pp. 83-236.

5. Ibid. pp. 303-336.

6. Ibid. p. 348.

7. Leonardo Boff, *Church: Charism and Power* (New York: Crossroad, 1985), p. 139.

8. Osborne, *Priesthood,* pp. 330-333; see also David N. Power, who speaks of the "growing appreciation of the collegiality of the ordained priesthood" in his *Ministers of Christ and His Church* (London: Geoffrey Chapman, 1969), p. 189.

9. David N. Power, *Ministers of Christ and His Church,* p. 183.

10. Anglican-Roman Catholic International Commission, *Final Report* (London: CTS/SPCK, 1982).

11. WCC, *Baptism, Eucharist and Ministry* (Geneva: WCC, 1982).

12. Roman Catholic-Lutheran Joint Commission, *Facing Unity: Models, Forms and Phases of Catholic-Lutheran Church Fellowship* (Geneva: Lutheran World Federation, 1985).

13. These documents can be found in *Growth in Agreement: Reports and Agreed Statements of Ecumenical Conversations on a World Level,* eds. Harding Meyer and Lukas Vischer (New York: Paulist Press, 1984), pp. 168-189.

14. Published in *Facing Unity,* pp. 72-79.

15. *A Plan of Union for the Church of Christ Uniting* (Princeton: COCU, 1985).

16. See John A. Rodano, "Consultation on Church Union: Recent Developments, New Directions," *Religious Studies Review* 11 (1985) 155.

17. *The COCU Consensus: In Quest of a Church of Christ Uniting,* Gerald F. Moede (Princeton, COCU, 1985).

18. Anglican-Lutheran Consultation, *Niagara Report* (London: Church Publishing House, 1988).

19. *Ministry and Ordination* (no. 9), in *Final Report.*

20. *Lumen Gentium*, no. 25, in Walter Abbott, *The Documents of Vatican II* (New York: America Press, 1966), pp. 47-50.

21. See the remarks of the research team appointed by the Catholic Theological Society of America in "A Global Evaluation of Baptism, Eucharist and Ministry" in *Catholic Perspectives on Baptism, Eucharist and Ministry*, ed. Michael A. Fahey (Lanham: University Press of America, 1986), p. 24.

22. Cf. William Marrevee, "Lima Document on Ordained Ministry," in Fahey, *Catholic Perspectives*, p. 175.

23. Geoffrey Wainwright, "Reconciliation in Ministry," in *Ecumenical Perspectives on Baptism, Eucharist and Ministry*, ed. Max Thurian (Geneva: WCC, 1983), p. 132.

24. Kenan Osborne notes that the limits of papal authority vis-à-vis the sacramental nature of the episcopacy is an issue that still needs clarification, *Priesthood*, p. 341.

25. Cited in *The Los Angeles Times*, March 23, 1991, F 17.

26. As reported by William Carpe in an editorial, *Ecumenical Trends* 20 (April 1991) 50.

27. Cf. Thomas P. Rausch, S.J., *Authority and Leadership in the Church* (Wilmington: Michael Glazier, 1989), pp. 67-69.

6. PRIESTHOOD IN THE CHURCH: SOME CONCLUSIONS

In this study of priesthood in the contemporary church we have examined and appraised various models of priesthood. We have asked what it means to minister as a priest at this moment in the life of the church and have examined the place of affectivity in the life of a priest. We have sought to describe more accurately the nature of priesthood in apostolic religious communities. Finally, we have considered the role of the bishop who receives the fullness of the priesthood. Now it is time to draw together our conclusions.

1. From the time of the New Testament prophets and teachers, the church's ministry of leadership has included both prophetic and cultic elements. Though the New Testament does not speak of ordained ministers as priests, from very early in the Christian tradition the language of priesthood (*hiereus, sacerdos, sacerdotium*) has been used of the bishop, in recognition of his unique role as the minister and leader of the eucharistic community. And by extension, it came to be used of his assistants, the presbyters. The English word "priest" is derived ultimately from the New Testament term "presbyter."

2. Some expressions of the church's priesthood have been more cultic in orientation. Monastic priests whose lives are devoted to the divine praise and worship exercise a priesthood focused on the *opus Dei* and the liturgy. Secular or diocesan priests typically exercise a ministry of word, sacrament, and pastoral leadership within a local church community, on either a parish or a diocesan level.

3. Religious priests belonging to communities founded for an apostolic preaching ministry beyond the confines of a local church (Dominicans, Franciscans, Jesuits, etc.) exercise a priesthood which was originally more prophetic in orientation. Their priesthood was given to the ministry of the word in its fullest sense; it came to include not just preaching and sacramental celebration, but a dedication to the ministries of interiority and social justice. There is still a need in the church for such a prophetic or kerygmatic priesthood, particularly in the areas of evangelization, social justice, higher education, and the intellectual apostolate.

4. At the same time there is a prophetic dimension to the ministry of every priest. The mission of a priest includes preaching and teaching. But a priest who is not formed and reshaped interiorly by the power of the word cannot hope to preach and teach effectively. Priests need to live from the word of God, like Jeremiah, the reluctant prophet who nevertheless experienced the word like a fire burning in his heart and imprisoned in his bones (Jer 20:9). They must imitate Jesus whose own life moved ever more deeply into the mystery of the one he called Abba.

A priest today who loses the prophetic dimension of his priesthood does so at great cost to himself. His priesthood can easily become one of mere ritualism, the expression of a cultic religion at the expense of the messianic discipleship proclaimed by Jesus.

5. The sacral concept of priesthood which emerged in the middle ages represents a one-sided emphasis on the cultic role of the priest, particularly in the celebration of the eucharist. It is not an adequate model for understanding the priesthood. The priest is not a sacred person; nor can priesthood be adequately understood simply in terms of the priest's eucharistic role apart from the relationship of the priest to a community. Still, gathering the community in prayer and presiding at its eucharistic table remains essential to the office of the priest.

6. The emphasis on priesthood as ministry (*diakonia*) has helped recover the image of the priest as a servant leader who must model his own ministry on the example of Jesus' loving service of others. For priests today that means a certain vulnerability, giving up any privilege based on office or status. It means exercising a ministry of reconciliation such as Jesus exemplified in his tradition of table fellowship. It means a ministry of leadership which is collaborative and empowering rather than dominative, able both to share and to articulate the experience of others, and at the same time to challenge them.

Affectivity plays an important role in the life of a priest precisely as a minister. A priest whose celibacy cuts him off from affective relationships with other people cannot imitate Jesus' example of loving service. A celibacy which keeps others at a safe distance may keep a priest from being vulnerable, but it is not an expression of the discipleship that gospel celibacy represents.

7. Important as the ministerial model is, it does not address the question of what is specific to the ministry of the priest. The representational model does this. By ordination the priest is authorized to speak in the name of the church and in certain cases to act in Christ's name. Thus

the priest becomes a public person in the church, one who acts *in persona Christi* (LG 28).

The representational model moves beyond a strictly functional definition of priesthood without placing the ordained minister on a higher level of being than other members of the faithful. Like all the baptized, priests must strive to make transparent in their own lives the grace of their baptism.

8. The Second Vatican Council returned to the understanding of priesthood and orders familiar to the ancient church. *Lumen Gentium* ascribes the fullness of the priesthood to the bishop (LG 21, 26, 28). In the rite of ordination to the presbyterate, revised after the council, the prayer of consecration asks that the ordinand might receive "the dignity of the order of presbyters...the second order of the hierarchy."

But the council also saw a more personal relationship of interdependence between a bishop and his priests. Priests are "cooperators" with the episcopal order and "coworkers" with the bishop (LG 28). They should be regarded as counselors to the bishop and should be able to look on the bishop in a special way as their pastor.

9. From the ecumenical dialogues comes a recognition of the bishop's responsibility for symbolizing and maintaining the communion of the local church with the apostolic church and with the worldwide communion of churches which constitutes the church catholic. The meaning of the Catholic emphasis on apostolic succession can be found here. While there is an increasing readiness to accept the office of bishop in the dialogues, it is clear that without a reform of the way that episcopal authority is exercised, such an office will not be accepted.

By their communion with the bishop, priests also symbolize and maintain the communion that exists between the local congregation and the worldwide communion of the church. This is particularly true when the priest presides at the eucharist; at this moment the nature of the church confessed and lived out as one, holy, catholic, and apostolic comes to expression.

10. This study has focused on priesthood in the church today. Because of this focus, it has prescinded from a number of questions being raised in the contemporary church, among them the questions of clerical celibacy and the ordination of women. The church's priesthood has assumed a number of different forms and expressions in the past. What forms and expressions it will take in the future remains to be seen.

INDEX OF NAMES